S0-AIM-486

Publisher's Message

The most basic premise of Lean is to *simply* and effectively problem solve. Today it appears organizations may be focusing too much time on training everyone in the words, tools, concepts, etc. of Lean (or commonly known as the Toyota Production System) while not including many of the fundamental problem solving and quality improvement tools that will help sustain any and all Lean initiatives. This burst of Lean training may be confusing to the employees, disgruntling them, or it may not be allowing them to attain a level of understanding necessary to assist in the issue at hand. It *may* be of more value to teach the basic Lean tool of problem solving first (i.e., the PLAN - DO - CHECK - ACT (PDCA)) methodology with a Lean perspective and then progress into more advanced Lean tool training. *The Simply Lean Pocket Guide* is a step-by-step approach to the implementation of process improvements using the PDCA model along with a Lean focus.

If you are just beginning to adopt Lean or Six Sigma as a business improvement model, whether you are in the healthcare, financial services, construction, armed services, manufacturing, government, logistics, service, or construction industry, the first thing that should be acknowledged is that the solution to the problem (or improvement target that is to be reached) will be found in the intellect of the people who are working the process. Therefore, as a trainer, consultant (internal or external), or departmental head, the focus to improve a situation would be to "somehow" work with that group (and their intellect) and find a solution. However, that "somehow" is not always easy to attain and will require some guidance along the way. *Simply Lean* will provide that guidance ensuring root causes and wastes are eliminated in creating a Leaner, problem-free process.

During the many workshops that I have conducted throughout the years, I am commonly asked, "Isn't Lean just common sense?" And, to them I emphatically say, "Yes!". And for that individual the light bulb has gone off and they have taken a giant leap in their Lean understanding. *Simply Lean* was published to assist this "light bulb" in going off in more people in your organization

This practice and understanding of the tools in this book should be the first step in any Lean journey. It is the challenge of the trainer, coach, champion, consultant, manager, etc. (whomever is responsible for the problem solving, Lean or Six Sigma project) to facilitate the improvement process with a course of action that will attain the goals set. *This book is not about teaching the Lean tools of 5S, Mistake Proofing, Visual Controls, JIT, etc. - there is plenty of material already published on those topics - but it is a book to more fully engage the process worker with a revisit of the quality improvement tool set with just a twist of Lean.*

Wherever you are in your Lean journey, this book will assist you to accelerate improvement initiatives to the next level. *Simply Lean* is about revisiting the PLAN-DO-CHECK-ACT (PDCA) cycle of problem solving with a long term Lean focus and direction. Toyota's success is not found so much in their full blown, week-long, detailed kaizen events, but in the power of their employees to *simply* problem solve.

Don Tapping
Publisher

Purpose of this Pocket Guide

This pocket guide was created to provide the necessary forms and worksheets for a team to learn, implement, and document Lean problem solving activities using the PLAN-DO-CHECK-ACT (PDCA) methodology. PDCA is a cycle of activities designed to drive continuous improvement. Initially implemented in manufacturing, it has broad applicability in business. First developed by Walter Shewhart, it was popularized by Dr. W. Edwards Deming. The activities surrounding the training and implementation of the PDCA methodology will be referred to as a PDCA Kaizen Event (see next section). Lean tools and concepts will be briefly referenced where appropriate to assist the overall Lean training process.

Problems (or areas for improvement) can be identified via a current state value stream map, process map, customer mandate, or by negative trends from a Balance Scorecard. This book will also provide space to document individual "Idea Kaizen" activities. An "Idea Kaizen" is a suggestion that is beyond the scope of the current project but is documented to be considered for an individual implementation activity at a later date.

This book will assist teams and individuals to:

- ✔ Collect the right data, in the right way, to support Lean or Six Sigma projects
- ✔ Meet effectively to maximize organizational resources
- ✔ Brainstorm to solicit best ideas
- ✔ Obtain a consensus to solve problems and determine solutions
- ✔ Determine root cause(s)
- ✔ Standardize improvements
- ✔ Think outside the box
- ✔ Accept change
- ✔ Work to attain process perfection

This pocket guide was designed to be:

1. **A standard problem solving guide.** To ensure the best use of everyone's time, this guide will provide the basic structure (i.e., standard) for which all Lean or Six Sigma teams should follow (or supplement your existing Lean or problem solving training). By using time wisely, it will reduce the variation in the overall continuous improvement process and provide a solid foundation upon which to introduce additional Lean tools.

2. **A reference guide for the problem solving tools.** Short, concise definitions of a tool, along with an example, will allow a team member to reference the tool when needed - especially when that team member is away from the team collecting data or working on a pilot project as part of the event.

3. **A learning tool.** A case study called "Tinker Town" is presented throughout this book to provide examples of how the various tools are used, as well as their relativity to Lean. This case study will assist you to better understand how to use a particular tool in your project.

4. **A team and personal log.** Notes and ideas about the area or process that is being analyzed can be easily written down in this book so as not to lose or misplace valuable process information. Your Idea Kaizens can also be recorded in the appropriate section of this book. Pages for your note taking are designated by the pen icon.

*It is acknowledged that the areas provided throughout this book for you to write in are somewhat limiting, however, these worksheets can be created in Microsoft Word or Excel. Larger worksheets are provided in the Appendix. They are also available in Microsoft Excel at **www.theleanstore.com.***

A Lean Overview

The Toyota Production System (TPS) is used synonymously with Lean or continuous improvement throughout the world. It is based on continually meeting customer requirements efficiently and effectively with little or no waste. Waste is considered the non value-added activities that the customer should not, and will not, pay for.

Lean is a compilation of world-class practices adapted from the United States, Japan, and Germany. Today, in Japan, they refer to Just-In-Time as JIT - an American acronym. Similarly, takt, a German word, refers to "beat" or "rhythm". The important point to understand is that Lean has had a global birth; practitioners need not get caught up in whether a particular word or phrase is American, German, or Japanese.

The traditional model had an organization continually increasing prices to its customers, until the 1990s when customers began demanding price reductions. As material prices increased, as well as healthcare costs and employee wages, the only way to satisfy the customers' demands and keep their business was to adopt Lean techniques. This "new" customer would not pay for waste in the processes and was very astute in determining what the cost should be. Therefore, companies had to focus on their internal costs to maintain current business and be in better position for additional business opportunities. The following illustration demonstrates the Traditional Thinking and Lean Thinking models:

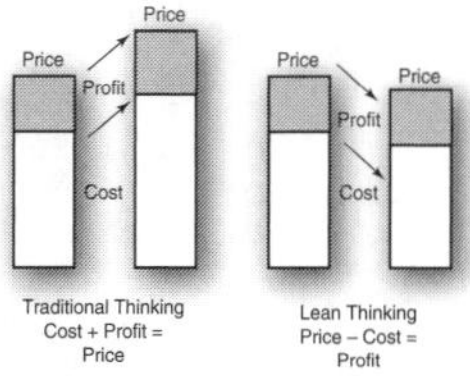

The Lean Thinking model has the identification and elimination of waste as a primary objective. Problem solving, as well as the other Lean tools, will assist in the process.

The seven wastes are:

1. Overproduction
This waste is producing some type of product or providing a service prior to it being required. This is the greatest of all the wastes. In that, if you overproduce some type of work or service, it encompasses many of the other wastes.

2. Waiting (Time-In-Queue)
Waiting for anything (people, signatures, information, etc.) is waste. This waste of waiting is considered "low hanging fruit" because it is easy to get and ripe for the taking.

3. Motion
Any movement of people, paper, electronic exchanges (e-mails, etc.) that does not add value is waste. This waste can be created by poor office layout or design, ineffective office equipment, or supplies located afar.

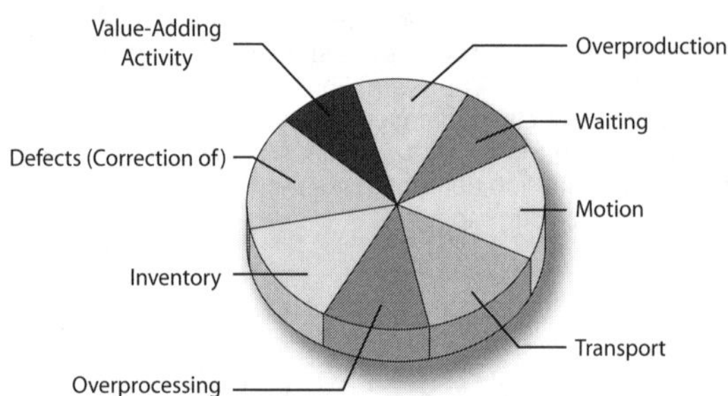

4. Transport (or conveyance)
Transport is an important and ubiquitous element. It affects the delivery of any work within the office or to and from a customer.

5. Overprocessing
Putting more resources than necessary into the work required by the internal or external customer is waste.

6. Inventory
Excess time, work piles, and excess supplies are waste. They all take up space or time, and may become obsolete or not used if customer requirements change. Time can also be considered inventory.

7. Defects (Corrrection of)
This category of waste refers to all processing required to correct a defect. Defects (either internal or external) result in additional administrative processes that will add no value to the product or service.

(8.) People's Skills (People Utilization)
You will sometimes find an eighth waste, people utilization. This waste is not utilizing people's skills to their fullest.

While you progress through the PDCA methodology, utilize the Waste Audit that is contained in the Appendix of this book. This is usually done in the Plan phase.

The concept and practices of Lean are a system of Just-In-Time delivery of goods and/or services, with no errors (Jidoka or Mistake Proofing - building quality in). The heart of the system is employee involvement, making waste elimination a day-by-day and minute-by-minute activity. For a Lean house to be built, the foundation of process stabilization and standardization must be present. And for this to occur, problem solving should be utilized.

The Customers

It is through management commitment (and involvement), employee training, and effective communications that a customer-focused Lean house can be built.

Internal or external customers will benefit from all Lean actions through the implementation of PDCA Kaizen Events and/or Idea Kaizens. It is with this customer focus that separates Lean from many other types of business improvement methodologies. A Lean concept known as a value stream map may serve as a catalyst to identify the PDCA Kaizen Events.

The value stream map allows for a clear understanding of the various processes, comprised of both value-added and non value-added activities, that satisfy a customer demand. A value stream map is a visual representation of all this information. It typically would connect the external customer (i.e., the customer, client, member, or patient), through all the internal customers of an organization, to the various suppliers (i.e., those that supply goods and services to the organization). However, many times the flow of goods and/or services encounter bottlenecks (approvals, regulations, other departmental processes, attitudes, etc.) within the organization along the way.

Lean (i.e., through effective problem solving) can be used to eliminate these bottlenecks so goods and/or services can flow seamlessly.

The platforms or formats in which to eliminate these bottlenecks are referred to as kaizen activities. There are two types of kaizen activities discussed in this book, the PDCA Kaizen Event and the Idea Kaizen.

A Twist of Lean

Problem solving is a process or methodology used to permanently solve undesirable process variations (i.e., eliminate waste) or conditions. By definition, a "problem" exists when a process that has been producing acceptable results begins producing unacceptable results.

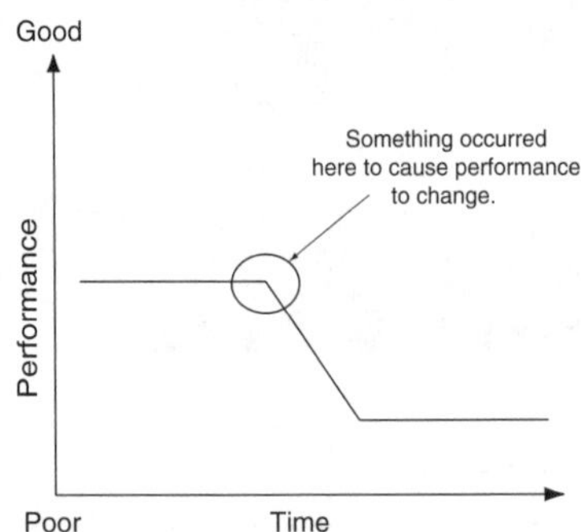

It is the goal of this book to provide a team that has been designated with solving a problem to not only ensure the process attains its previous performance measures, but with some Lean practices, improve the process to another level. For example, let's say a team is working on a customer service problem solving project. The customer survey results had recently declined the past few months, which resulted in a loss of sales. The team could follow the problem solving (PDCA) methodology (or similar method) and solve the problem to get back to where they were previously. However, if the team understood some basic concepts of:

1. Takt time (i.e., knowing exactly the number of orders being received per day in customer service)
2. Pitch (how often does work or orders need to move to to the next process for continuous flow to occur)

3. Visual controls (how capacity issues can be identified throughout the day when customer service representatives are getting behind)
4. Mistake Proofing (how preventing errors and mistakes can eliminate invoicing defects when orders are being entered)

...then improvements such as these could likely launch the team beyond the pre-problem solving process measurements. There are many more such "Lean" type questions that can be asked when solving a problem. However, keep the use and application of any Lean tools **simple**!

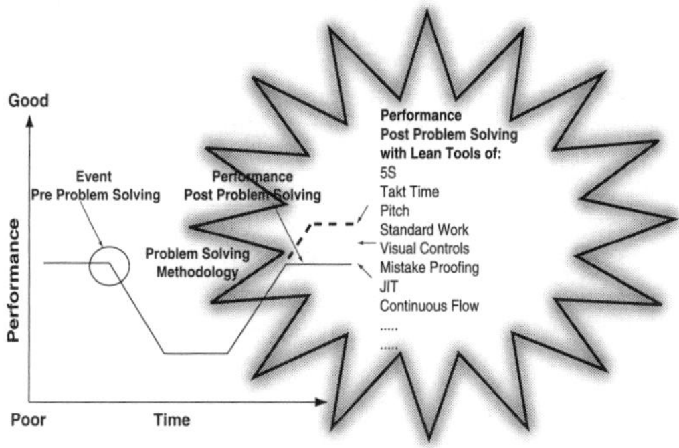

A Lean tool known as a PDCA Kaizen Event is a method you can use to implement Lean in your problem solving project.

Kaizens

Kaizen is derived from the word "kai" which means to "take apart" and "zen" which means to "make good". Kaizen is also synonymous with continuous improvement.

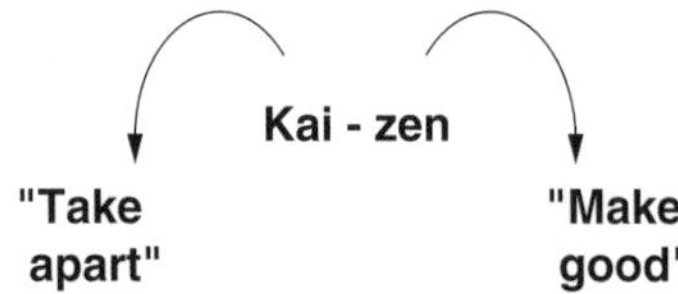

Kaizen can be major organizational improvements directed to an entire value stream (i.e., integrating two business units' processes) or it can be something very simple (i.e., placing a Post-it Note on a signature page to make sure a document is signed in the right location) - and everything in-between.

The Simply Lean Pocket Guide explains two different types of kaizens to assist you in this process - the PDCA Kaizen Event and the Idea Kaizen.

PDCA Kaizen Event

The PDCA Kaizen Event is comprised of using standard problem solving methodology tools (i.e., fishbones, pareto analysis, 5 Whys, countermeasures, etc.) with a consideration and use of basic Lean tools and practices. PDCA Kaizen Events will provide a structured approach once target improvement areas have been identified via a value stream or process map, negative trends from a Balanced Scorecard, or by some process attributes that have deviated from their expected performance.

The PDCA Kaizen cycle is designed to be used as a dynamic continuous improvement model - allowing the energy (i.e., the ideas and possible solutions) from one phase to continue to the next. The cycle will ensure that the root cause (i.e., the waste) is identified and subsequently create the correct plan to put the proper measures in place to eliminate the root cause. However, if the problem persists (i.e., the root cause was not identified correctly or no controls implemented), then the cycle would repeat itself.

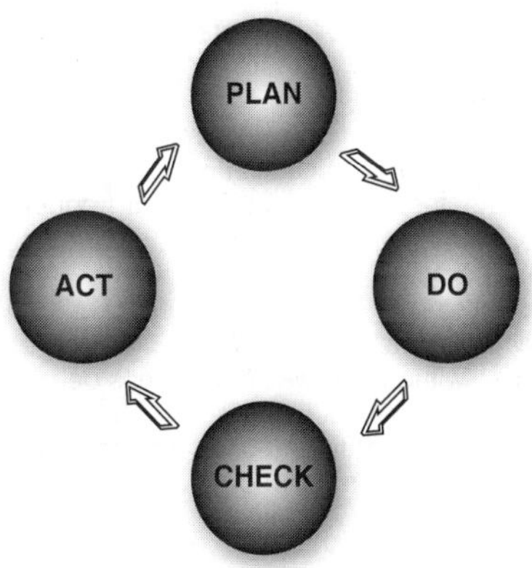

The four phases to the PDCA Kaizen Event are:

1. PLAN - ***to identify and analyze the problem.***

The first step in the PDCA Kaizen Event is to choose an area that offers the most return for the effort and will be the biggest bang for your buck - that "low-hanging" fruit. To identify these areas consider using a value stream map, flowchart (or process map), customer surveys, trends from a Balanced Scorecard, quarterly reports, code books, First Time Quality Reports, Incident Reports, audits, etc. Effective meetings, effective teams, problem identification, brainstorming, flowcharts, fishbones (cause and effect diagrams), data collection, and 5 Why analysis can be helpful in this phase. This is "What" the problem is and "Why" the problem is occurring. The following Lean questions may also stimulate ideas about the problem identified:

1. Is takt time (i.e., customer demand and net available time) known and understood?
2. Are the processes or process stabilized so the process output is predictable?
3. Are the processes or process standardized to best practice? And if so, is there a systematic process for improvement?
4. Are the processes or process simplified for easy cross-training or visual communications?
5. Are there defects or errors that occur frequently in the process?
6. Is there a process throughput issue?
7. Is there a capacity issue with the process?
8. Will people, material, and/or data flow more continuously (i.e., without the waste of excess delays, motion, etc.)?
9. Can people, material, and/or access to data be located in a more efficient location?

2. DO - *develop and implement a solution(s).*

Implement the change you decided on in the PLAN phase. Communicate to everyone affected by the change what is happening. Also, isolate any external customers from any and all potential problems that may be part of any trial that may have a negative impact. The Countermeasure Kaizen Log, Training Plan, and Gantt Chart can be helpful with this phase. The following Lean questions may also stimulate ideas about further developing a solution and/or implementing a trial:

1. Are there temporary resources available to ensure the customer (i.e., client, patient, etc.) is not affected by the trial, similar to a doctor's credo of "Do no harm"?
2. Are standard methods being used and documented to ensure uniformity in the overall improvement project?
3. Are there adequate visual controls to identify problems if they are still occurring?
4. Is data being collected at the process level that is related directly to the improvement (and made visible, if appropriate)?

3. CHECK - *to evaluate the results*.

In particular, what was learned and/or what went wrong? This is a crucial step in the PDCA cycle. Once you have implemented the change for a short time, you must determine how well it is working. Is it really the improvement that you had hoped? Decide on several measures with which you can monitor to gauge the level of improvement. Impact Maps and Run Charts can be helpful with this phase. The following Lean questions may also stimulate ideas about what went well and what needs to improve:

1. Did the visual controls work?
2. Did the standard work procedures get documented to the appropriate level?
3. Has the data supported the improvement(s)?

4. **ACT** - ***to adopt and/or update the necessary standards, abandon the process change, or run through the cycle again.***

After planning, implementing, and monitoring the change (improvement initiative) you must decide whether it is worth continuing the change that was done. If it consumed too much of your time, was difficult to adhere to, too expensive in resource allocations or costs, or even led to no improvement, you may consider abandoning the change and planning a new one. However, if the change led to a desirable improvement or outcome, you would expand the changes to a system or enterprise-wide implementation. The following Lean questions may also stimulate ideas about what more needs to be done:

1. Have Standard Work procedures been created for the improved process? Are they visual, easy-to-use?
2. Has a timeline been created to roll-out the improvements to other areas or departments (if appropriate)?
3. Is everyone being trained to the new process?
4. Is data being collected and analyzed (i.e., control charts, etc.) with the improvements over a 7 - 30 - 60 day window to ensure the PDCA Kaizen Event improvements are sustained?

This was a brief overview of the PDCA Kaizen Event cycle. Use this as a guide in your problem solving, Lean, and/or Six Sigma project.

Important Note: *The various tools that comprise the PDCA Kaizen Event listed in the previous few pages serve only as a guide. Many times the same tool will be used in another phase. For example, brainstorming is probably used in all phases to solicit input for ideas on solutions or why solutions did not work. Data Check Sheets are also likely to be used in all phases because process data continually needs to be collected and reviewed.*

A3 Report - Storyboard

The following two page spread is a convenient and efficient way to display all the relevant information from your PDCA Kaizen Event on a single sheet of paper (11" x 17"). Toyota refers to this as an A3 report. It is also commonly referred to as a Storyboard. Do not use it just at the end of the project, use it at every step to visually convey the team's progress. Storyboards are dynamic and should be updated regularly by posting in the location that the kaizen action is being conducted.

The Storyboard is the framework for holding all key information for a problem solving or Lean project. It is organized into various areas that can be represented by simple illustrations (i.e., fishbones, paretos, photos, etc.).

Storyboard (A3 Report)

PDCA Kaizen Project Name: ______________________

Team Members: ______________________

Problem Identification

WHO: ______________________
WHAT: ______________________
WHERE: ______________________
WHY: ______________________
HOW: ______________________
QUANTITY: ______________________

Data Chart of Present Condition

(from Data Check Sheet and/or Pareto)

Goal / Standard

____

Waste(s) Indentified

- ❐ Overproduction
- ❐ Waiting
- ❐ Motion
- ❐ Transport
- ❐ Overprocessing
- ❐ Inventory (Time)
- ❐ Defects (Correction of)
- ❐ People's Skills

Measurement(s) Affected

__________ __________

Fishbone

Counter

(Actions from the

Interim Containment Actions

MAN

MATERIAL

MACHINE

METHOD

Storyboard (A3 Report)

Date: ______________________

Value Stream: ______________

Diagram	Results
	BEFORE AFTER

measures 5 Why analysis) Permanent Countermeasure Actions	Standardization
	Yokoten Review Date
	Recognition
	Next Target

Many organizations will create an Excel spreadsheet with a similar format as shown. Additional tabs (or the back side of the hardcopy paper report) can be used to communicate 5 Why Analysis, photos, etc. Consider laminating the hardcopy sheet to be displayed at the Yokoten. A Yokoten is a sharing of information throughout an organization. It is a form of knowledge management.

Storyboard (A3 Report)
Page 2

Identifying Root Causes (Brainstorming)

	Possible Causes	Verification
MAN		
MACHINE		
METHOD		
MATERIAL		
OTHER		

Any information to help clarify the problem, show root causes, verify countermeasures, etc. can be displayed someplace on the Storyboard. Another way to organize the information is by the 5W's and 2H's (Who? What? Where? Why? When? and How? and How Much?). Use (and improve upon) what is more common to your organization to build upon existing training and experience.

Storyboard (A3 Report) Page 2

Fishbone **(other worksheets as appropriate)**

Impact Map **(other worksheets as appropriate)**

Idea Kaizen

The Idea Kaizen is a quick and easy method to document and solve a simple problem. This is an on-the-spot type problem solving and problem resolution activity requiring minimal resources and (typically) no management approval. The Idea Kaizen is similar in nature to an idea submitted in a company's Suggestion Program. The main difference is that in the Idea Kaizen employees are empowered and encouraged to make the change themselves, if at all possible. These changes (or improvements) should not have any negative impact on other parts of the organization.

It is the employees doing their job, working that process level detail (i.e., making a product, providing a service, or processing data) day in and day out that have the best ideas to reduce and eliminate waste. The Idea Kaizen is meant to engage those employees to gain additional ownership of their processes through documentation and sharing of Idea Kaizens. Once Idea Kaizens become a way of life for all employees within an organization, then a true continuous improvement culture will have emerged.

Note: Some Idea Kaizens may require a PDCA Kaizen Event. The important aspect of the Idea Kaizen is to document improvement ideas as they occur.

The following is an example of an Idea Kaizen. Additional Idea Kaizen Forms are located in the Appendix to be separated and photocopied for use.

Idea Kaizen Form

Name: Will Robinson Department: Customer Service

Upstream Customer: Sales Downstream Customer: Distribution

Step 1: Describe the Problem. Date: 9/15

Include photos, charts, and graphs, if necessary.

The current discount schedule for Gilmore Industries is not current. The last two invoices were incorrect and the customer was not pleased.

Step 2: Describe the Action to be Taken. Date: 9/15

Include photos, charts, and graphs, if necessary.

The new sales manager was informed of the standard procedure for updating customer discounts. Distribution was also notified of this change to ensure the correct invoice was shipped with the products. The IT department created a link between the two departments to ensure the discount would automatically be reflected.

Step 3: Follow-up. Did the Action Work? ■ Yes ☐ No Date: 9/30

Include photos, charts, and graphs, if necessary.

Additional Notes:

All invoices were correct for Gilmore Industries. IT initiated a verfication process to ensure all other customers had a similar process.

The following listing compares the basic attributes of the Idea Kaizen and PDCA Kaizen.

Idea Kaizen	PDCA Kaizen
✔ On-the-spot type solutions ✔ Similar to submitting an idea in a company's Suggestion Program ✔ Few resources required (time, people, etc.) ✔ Not requiring value stream mapping ✔ Not as structured ✔ May be a "quick-fix" ✔ Not as detailed ✔ Root cause may or may not be found ✔ Common sense solution ✔ Requires only the individual (or 1 other person) for implementation ✔ May require the PDCA Kaizen process	✔ Requires a cross-functional team ✔ Typically identified as a waste on a value stream map ✔ Structured process ✔ Tools of Fishbone, Pareto, and Countermeasures typicallly used ✔ Identifies root cause(s) ✔ Requires good data collection ✔ Can be tied directly to stakeholder loyalty, cash generation, and/or return on investment

Please see page 217 for forms to assist in the planning and reporting of your PDCA Kaizen Event.

How to Use this Pocket Guide

This pocket guide is:

1. **A quick-reference guide.** Problem solving and Lean tools are explained in more detail in other manuals and/or by your facilitator during the instruction portion of the workshop. However, many times team members will require a short, concise reminder of the tool - especially when they are away from the team collecting process data or working on a pilot project as part of the event. This pocket guide will serve as that quick-reference guide.

2. **A learning tool.** Throughout the PDCA Kaizen Event portion of this pocket guide examples from an actual Kaizen Event will be used to demonstrate many of the tools that are common in problem solving and Lean/Six Sigma projects. The case study will allow you to better understand and learn about each tool prior to potential application in your Kaizen Event. Keep in mind, even though the examples from the case study are not identical to your specific application, they will guide you in the right direction in using that tool.

3. **Your workbook toolkit.** The "how to" instructions, along with the allocated workspace, allow each team member to document the PDCA Kaizen Event as it is progressing. This will be helpful in reviewing information when determining root cause. It will allow everyone to *continually* be on the same page.

4. **Your personal Kaizen planner.** PDCA Kaizen Events typically will have tasks assigned to each team member that are expected to be completed prior to the next meeting. Many of these tasks (i.e., action items) will need to be organized and planned into the daily activities of the person's current work schedule. This pocket guide will serve as an individual planner. The Countermeasure Kaizen Log allows each team member to list those action items that are assigned, as well as the deadline by which they will need to be completed.

5. **A tool to self-initiate additional Idea Kaizens.** Throughout a PDCA Kaizen Event you most likely will identify additional opportunities of how waste can be eliminated that are beyond the scope of the current PDCA Kaizen Event. Those additional ideas for improvement should be captured in the Idea Kaizen section of this book.

6. **An A3 Report or Storyboard template.** An A3 Report or Storyboard is the graphical representation of the project on one sheet of paper. By using the template contained in this workbook, it will assist you in displaying all key parts of the Kaizen Event.

7. **A self-paced preparation guide.** After each phase there is a Readiness Guide that consists of a series of questions to prepare you for the next phase.

PDCA Lean Tool Usage Matrix

The following PDCA Lean Tool Usage Matrix represents typical problem solving tools, as well as a good sample of Lean tools and concepts. Checkmarks have been placed in the appropriate column as a *guide* to their usage within the PDCA Kaizen Event cycle. The purpose of this matrix is to convey that:

a) Many of the tools can be used anytime throughout the PDCA Kaizen Event process

b) If the PLAN phase is not done thoroughly, it may compromise the entire Kaizen Event

c) Most Lean tools should be reviewed in the PLAN phase to ensure their potential application and usage throughout the PDCA Kaizen Event process

d) There is a correlation between effectively following the PDCA methodology and the long-term engagement of the process worker in the Lean-Six Sigma journey

Keep in mind that the PDCA Lean Tool Usage Matrix is only a general reference.

PDCA - Lean

PDCA - Lean Tool	PLAN	DO	CHECK	ACT
5S	✓			
5 Why Analysis	✓	✓	✓	
Accepting Change	✓	✓	✓	✓
Brainstorming	✓	✓	✓	✓
Continuous Flow	✓			
Cycle Time	✓			
Data Collection	✓	✓	✓	✓
Effective Meetings	✓	✓	✓	✓
Effective Team	✓	✓	✓	✓
Failure Prevention Analysis	✓	✓	✓	
Fishbone	✓	✓	✓	
Flowchart	✓			
Gantt Chart		✓	✓	✓
Heijunka - Leveling	✓			
Idea Kaizen	✓	✓	✓	✓
Impact Map	✓	✓	✓	✓
Just-In-Time	✓			

Tool Usage Matrix

PDCA - Lean Tool				
Mistake Proofing	✓	✓	✓	
Paper File System	✓			
Pareto	✓		✓	
Performance Measurement	✓	✓	✓	✓
Physical Layout: U-shaped	✓			
Pitch	✓			
Problem Identfication	✓			
Pull Systems	✓			
Run Chart			✓	
Runners	✓			
Standard Work	✓			
Storyboard (A3 Report)	✓	✓	✓	✓
Takt Time	✓			
Training Plan	✓	✓		
Value Stream Mapping	✓			
Visual Controls	✓	✓	✓	✓
Waste Audit	✓			
Work Load Balancing	✓			
Yokoten				✓

Tool Overview

The following illustration previews the sequence of how the tools are implemented in the forthcoming case study. Please note, this is only one way that a problem can be solved with these tools and provides a guide for consideration in your problem solving, Lean, and/or Six Sigma project.

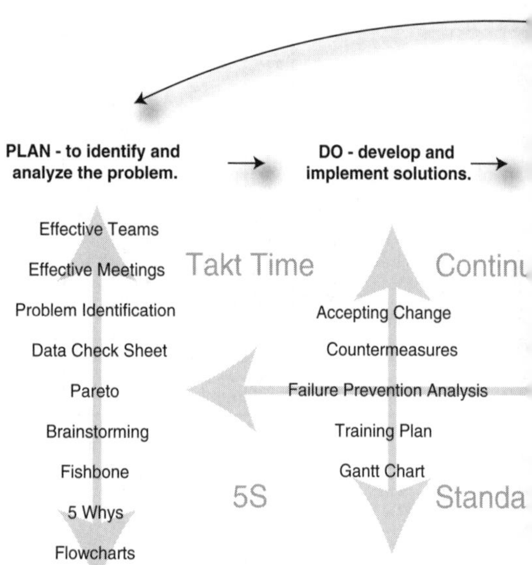

Denotes the inter-relatedness of the tools and their possible usage. included in the PLAN phase. Also, Brainstorming is typically done

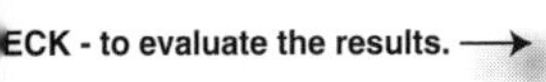

ECK - to evaluate the results. →

ACT- to adopt and/or update the necessary standards, abandon the process change, or run through the cycle again.

s Flow

Visual Controls

Impact Map

Run Chart

Standard Work

Performance Measurement

Yokoten

Work

Mistake Proofing

For example, Performance Measurement could have been in nearly every phase. Use this as only a guide!

The Case Study

The next few pages detail a case study that will be used throughout this pocket guide to demonstrate many of the tools. This is based on an actual case study. Certain aspects of the case study have been simplified for demonstration purposes. Questions will be provided that will stimulate ideas on how certain Lean tools and concepts may be considered.

Kate Mason, President and CEO, softly replaced the telephone receiver just as Jeff Stauer walked into her office.

"Well," Kate said, "That was the Baby Bundles purchasing manager and they're not renewing their order for Bright Baby Bears. 'Too many complaints,' they said. That was a custom design for their chain and their not renewing hurts."

"What'd you expect, given how our customer satisfaction ratings have dropped in the last two quarters?" Jeff asked.

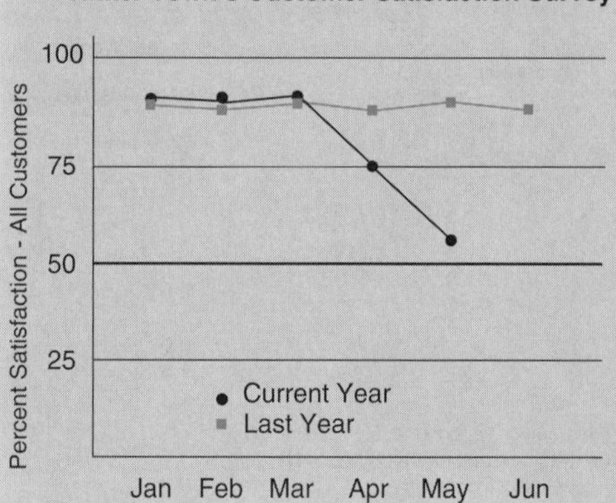

"What do you know that I don't know?" she asked.

"Nothing other than I actually read the reports I produce," he said.

"Our business is cyclical. You're new with the company. Look, there are always wobbles in customer satisfaction."

"This isn't a wobble. It's a ski slope," Jeff said. "The second monthly decline was predictable since we didn't do anything to correct the negatives that showed up in the preceding monthly report."

Kate kept her temper in check. It'd already been a bad morning. Baby Bundles' rejection had stunned her and what Jeff had said was true. She hadn't paid enough attention to the reports.

"You're right, Jeff. Could you please get me copies of those reports?"

Tinker Town, Inc. is a small manufacturer of all types of Teddy Bears, from the Standard Teddy Bear to customized ones for birthdays, holidays, country-type, and sports. The company is located in the southern part of the state, Santa Claus, Indiana. Tinker Town, Inc. has been in existence for over 50 years with an excellent name in the market place for quality. The Standard Teddy Bear was the original Teddy Bear and is still the most popular one to date. Tinker Town had always prided itself on high customer survey results - typically averaging around 90+% throughout the years. The industry benchmark had been 85%.

Approximately three months ago, Tinker Town, Inc. decided to go global and created a merchant account for their web site which allowed them to receive orders via the internet. This involved installing a new fulfillment system. They also participated in the Google AdWords program giving them immediate access to customers throughout the world.

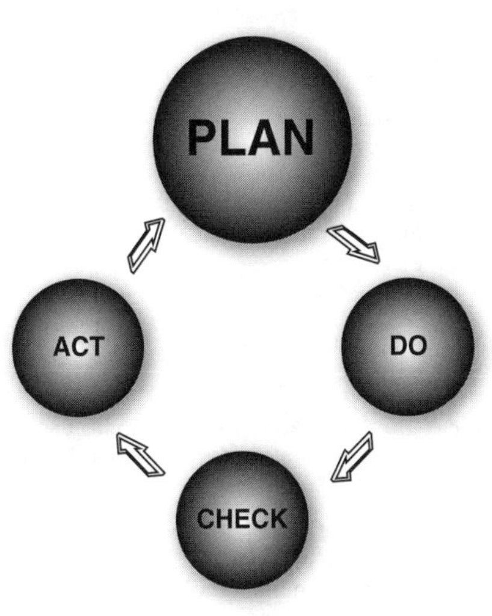
PLAN
DO
CHECK
ACT

PLAN - *to identify and analyze the problem*.

The PLAN phase of the PDCA Kaizen Event cycle is probably the most important step. It establishes the foundation upon which the team resources will be allocated. Therefore, the information collected and reviewed with the team must be complete and accurate.

In the PLAN phase, the following tools will be defined:

- ✔ Effective Teams
- ✔ Effective Meetings
- ✔ Problem Identification
- ✔ Brainstorming
- ✔ Flowchart
- ✔ Fishbone
- ✔ Data Collection
    - Data Check Sheet
    - Pareto Chart
- ✔ 5 Why Analysis

Note: These are the basic tools that can be used in the PLAN phase, however, they can also be used in the DO, CHECK, and ACT phases as well.

Note: While we are not attempting to teach the traditional Lean tools in this book, reference will be made to many of them. The references are meant to give additional insight into consideration of the Lean tool as a potential solution to the problem. For example, if there is a capacity issue in the customer service department for entering customer orders, and service levels have been declining for the past six months, then solving that problem may require the need to understand takt time (i.e., the customer demand, how many orders are being processed). The Glossary at the end of this book provides a brief description of each Lean tool.

Case Study - Effective Teams - Meeting 1

Kate met with Rita, the Quality Manager, and they went over Jeff's reports.

"I don't know what's happened," Rita said. "That's a poor statement from a quality manager but I'm mystified. I'll get right on this."

"No. First, I'm not blaming you. Second, I want us to implement Lean and we'll use this situation as our launching point for a new way to improve processes - I believe we can not only fix this problem, but create a new level of customer service."

Kate established a cross-functional Lean problem solving team made up of representatives from Marketing, Manufacturing, Customer Service, IT, Shipping and Receiving, Human Resources, and Rita. Kate, President and CEO, would be the Team Champion.

When the Lean team met for the first time, Juan Gonzales, the HR Manager, asked Kate, "Okay, so what do you want us to do?"

"Kate answered. "I don't have the answers but I think working as a group, we can come up with them. We can't just throw a bunch of people together and expect them to know how to function effectively as a team. We need to understand some basic principles about teaming and meeting effectively."

"That's a good point," Juan said. "I will schedule the training to be done before next week's meeting."

As Kate pointed out to Juan, too often, people are just thrown together and expected to perform as a team. That makes about as much sense as grabbing a bunch of football players and expecting them to play as a team. While the Lean tools and problem solving tools are obviously important, the key to Lean success is people working effectively together as a team.

The following information was conveyed at their next meeting, which was their initial training session.

Effective Teams

The PDCA Kaizen Event will not be successful without proper teaming. Understanding the basics of team dynamics will enhance the entire process by recognizing some basic do's and don'ts about working in groups.

The four stages of team development which each team will go through are:

Stage 1. Forming
Stage 2. Storming
Stage 3. Norming
Stage 4. Performing

Stage 1. Forming

The Forming stage of teaming involves reviewing the PDCA Kaizen project, establishing team roles, determining meeting times, and ensuring the right members are on the team.

This is the stage where team members experience difficulties from working as individuals to contributing as a team member. There is excitement, anticipation, and optimism. There is also the pride a member feels since he or she has been chosen. The "flip-side" are feelings of suspicion, fear, and anxiety about what is to come.

Additional points to consider at this initial stage are:

- Ensure roles are clearly defined and that a consensus is achieved on all decisions
- Rotate team member roles
- Conduct training activities on teaming or have some members attend a teaming workshop or seminar
- Establish team ground rules (i.e., turn cell phones off, be on time, etc.)

The Team Leader can remain in control by conducting effective meetings, using proper communications, and respecting team members' ideas.

Stage 2. Storming

At this stage, the team members begin to realize the task is different and/or more difficult than they first imagined. Impatience about the lack of progress and inexperience on group dynamics has some team members wondering about the entire project. Also, the team may experience some of the following:

- Continuing to rely on their personal experience of team projects and resist collaborating
- Arguing among members even when they agree on the real issue
- Being defensive and competitive

This stage can be difficult for any team. Teams that do not understand and acknowledge the four stages - especially this stage - most likely will disband.

The following ideas may assist teams through this stage:

- Constantly acknowledge the four stages with the team
- Communicate to the team that disagreements are part of the teaming process
- Focus on the Team Charter and goals
- Acknowledge progress to date
- Always focus on the process, not people or personalities
- Review team norms and standards before each meeting

If open resistance by one or two individuals occurs and creates an uncomfortable atmosphere for the team, a private meeting about this behavior with those individual(s) will need to be held.

Individual team members may lose the initial burst of excitement and energy exhibited from the Forming stage. Acknowledge this to the team and slowly focus on what can be done, by whom, and when it can be finished.

Stage 3. Norming

At this stage, team members accept the team concept. The team ground rules are being adhered to, communication is occurring without disruptions, and progress is being made toward the objective. At this stage, everyone feels that the team concept is working. Everyone is contributing in a positive way.

The team may also be doing some of the following:

- Expressing criticism constructively
- Attempting to achieve harmony by avoiding conflict
- Confiding in each other
- Exhibiting a sense of team togetherness

Continued communications and acknowledgement of the team members' efforts should be done often, allowing progression to Stage 4 and preventing the team from falling back to Stage 2.

Stage 4. Performing

By the time this stage has been reached the team can begin to diagnose and solve problems with relative ease. This stage includes:

- Making constructive self-changes
- Achieving project milestones earlier than anticipated
- Coaching by other team members in a support role

Teaming can be a challenge the first time. Utilizing the structured PDCA methodology will assist greatly in allowing the team to progress through all the stages without a major impact on the overall project.

Case Study - Effective Meetings - Meeting 1

The first half of the training was focused on teaming, with the second half to be focused on effective meetings."

Juan began the training session.

"We've all been involved in meetings. It's part of business life. However, far too many meetings are poorly run, waste people's time and don't accomplish significant goals. I'm going to cover the basics of effective meetings and then we can apply these principles to the Kaizen Event team we are all on."

Effective Meetings

Conducting effective meetings does not involve trial and error. It is critical to the efficiency of a PDCA Kaizen. An effective meeting is an efficient use of people's time when they are gathered together working to obtain a desired result. Meetings, like any process, can be studied and improved upon.

There are three keys to effective meetings:

1. Identifying *clear objectives* for meetings is similar to setting goals for any business improvement initiative.
2. There are rules and guidelines (i.e., *standards*) for conducting effective meetings.
3. *Total participation* by everyone must be present for an effective meeting.

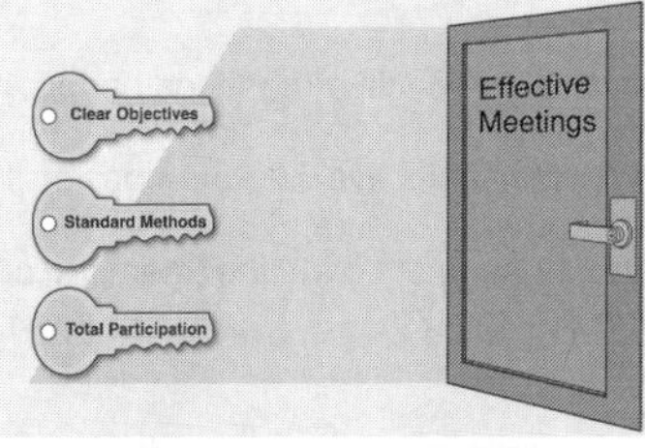

Why Effective Meetings Are Important

Meetings can be one of the most powerful business tools or one of the least. Common complaints about meetings are that:

- They accomplish nothing
- They are poorly organized
- Everyone has his or her own agenda
- They last too long
- People always arrive late
- No one is in control

However, people need to meet in order to benefit from the collective knowledge and experience of the group. While many decisions can be made by phone, e-mail, or in hallway discussions, there will be other times that people will need to meet and gain a consensus on an issue or problem that needs to be resolved. It is when this occurs that people gathered together need to meet *effectively.*

Effective meetings provide a forum to make necessary decisions and solve problems without wasting time. If meetings are effective, something positive will occur. They will produce a result. People will arrive on time, participate, offer information and ideas, and have a positive attitude. However, if meetings are not effective, people will show up late, they will be less likely to participate, and their attention and ideas will be less productive. To achieve effective meetings, treat them as processes, create standard rules to follow, and then adhere to those rules.

Approach conducting effective meetings as follows:

1. Agree on a clear objective and agenda for the meeting.
2. Choose the right people for the meeting and notify everyone in advance.

3. Clarify roles and responsibilities for the meeting (i.e., facilitator, scribe, team member, etc.).
4. Ensure everyone adheres to meeting etiquette (being on time, turning off cell phones/pagers, etc.).
5. Assign a scribe to take the meeting's minutes.
6. Assign a timekeeper to ensure the meeting stays on track.
7. Evaluate the meetings and improve where needed.
8. Provide minutes to participants within 24 hours after the meeting.

Note: It is important that the facilitator and scribe are not the same person.

The following page is the Effective Meeting Evaluation Worksheet that should be used:

1. Prior to any meeting to be reviewed by the PDCA facilitator. This will serve as their check sheet to make sure that the upcoming meeting is effective.

2. At the conclusion of the PDCA Kaizen Event by each team member. This will allow the facilitator to better understand how the meetings were conducted and serve as the basis for improving meeting effectiveness at the next PDCA Kaizen Event.

Use the following Effective Meeting Evaluation Worksheet with your team to continuously improve your meetings.

Effective Meeting Evaluation Worksheet 

Directions:

1. Spend only five minutes evaluating your meetings.
2. This form is most successful when everyone's responses are shared.
3. Focus on the weak spots, applaud the high ratings.

Rating System: 1 is the lowest score (Poor) and 5 is the highest (Excellent) **Poor** **Excellent** **1 2 3 4 5**	**Score**
1. How well did we stay on the agenda?	
2. Are we focusing on the right issues during the meeting?	
3. How well did we look for problems in the process, rather than the person?	
4. How well did we use our time?	
5. How well did we discuss information? How clearly? How accurately?	
6. How well did we all participate?	
7. Was the meeting effective?	
8. How was the pace, flow, and tone of the meeting? (Did we get bogged down or stuck?)	
9. How well did we respond to each other's questions and comments?	
10. In general, were all ideas explored to the extent possible given the time element?	
TOTAL:	
Please provide any other comments or suggestions for improvements.	

Problem Identification

This is the most crucial step and should not be rushed. The more specifically defined the problem is, the more likely the solution(s) will be effective.

Approach Problem Identification as follows:

1. Write a statement describing the problem. A good problem statement describes a situation both in terms of your own experience and in measurable terms.

2. Analyze the statement as to the following categories:

- Specific - What is it, and what is it not? How big is the problem? Is it increasing, decreasing, or unchanging?
- Time-bound - When did it first appear? How was it first identified? Are other events happening at the same time?
- Current - What is the present trend? Is it increasing, decreasing, or unchanging?

The Problem Identification Worksheet can be used to document the parameters of the problem. It is also referred to as an Is/Is Not analysis. The information that is obtained from the worksheet should be used to update the Team Charter. The Team Charter lists the deliverables required by the team (i.e., expected outcomes, timeframe, team member's names, etc.).

Case Study for Problem Identification - Meeting 1

The team decided to complete the Problem Identification Worksheet to clearly define the parameters of the problem. This allows them to tackle the problems that will provide them with the greatest return. This will ensure that they all agree on the exact nature of the problem before any resources are committed.

The following is their Problem Identification Worksheet.

Problem Identification Worksheet

Symptom: Customer complaints Date Opened: 6/1

Problem Description: The Customer Survey has gone from 90% (March) to 75% in April and 55% in May.

Waste Created: Defects, Motion Measurements Affected: Cash Generation, Profitability, Customer Sat. Survey

Is/Is Not Questions	IS	IS NOT
What **Object**	Customer Sat. Survey	Audits, quotes, etc.
Where **Seen on object**	Invoices	Quotes, expense reports, pick lists, etc.
When **First seen**	4/2	Prior to 4/2
When else seen	4/2 - 5/18	Prior to 4/2
How Large **How many objects have defects**	55% of surveys	45% of surveys
Trend **Increasing or decreasing over time**	Increasing	Decreasing

See pages 140-141 for a larger view of this worksheet.

Use the following Problem Identification Worksheet with your team to clearly define your problem.

Problem Identification Worksheet

Symptom:________________ Date Opened:____________

Problem Description:______________________________

____

Waste Created:____________ Measurements Affected:__________

Is/Is Not Questions	IS	IS NOT
What Object		
Where Seen on object		
When First seen When else seen		
How Large How many objects have defects		
Trend Increasing or decreasing over time		

Once you have completed this as best you can, write a brief problem statement for the Problem Description. This information should also be written on your Storyboard (pages 22-25).

Data Collection - Data Check Sheet

Data Check Sheets are used to collect, organize, prioritize, and analyze data. They can be used to answer the question, "How often is an event occurring?" They help to "see" the variations in the process. This information can be collected once a problem has been initially defined, or historical data can be used. The data collected should be easy to understand and provide a clearer picture of "the facts" as opposed to opinions of any team member.

When collecting data, decide who will collect the data, over what period, and from what sources. Make sure the data collected represents the results during a typical business cycle. Ensure all data is recorded, even if it may lead to redefining the problem or expanding the team's direction. Many times the data collected will be from the categories of a fishbone analysis activity. Note: Many times organizations have IT departments that can run reports and collect data that is pertinent to the problem that is to be solved. However, if additional process data at the source is required, use the same Data Collection Chart to organize and collect the information.

Approach creating a Data Check Sheet as follows:

1. Write the causes (typically derived from the fishbone analysis) on the left side.
2. Write the time span (hours, days, weeks, etc.) on the top of a horizontal sheet of paper, flipchart or whiteboard.
3. Determine how often the data will be collected.
4. Ensure data to be collected is easy to collect.
5. Collect data for a specified time period.
6. Continue with the PDCA Kaizen Event methodology.

Note: Data Check Sheets, as well as many of the other tools, can be used numerous times throughout a Kaizen Event. We are only demonstrating one use of each the tool in this case study.

Case Study for the Data Check Sheet - Meeting 1

The team decided to gather additional data specific to customer complaints to further prioritize what the reasons were for customers not being satisfied. From their experience, the typical reasons were due to incomplete shipment, incorrect price, wrong discount, and missed delivery. The team also decided to gather data on how many orders were being entered by customer service on a daily basis (i.e., determining takt time).

The following is their Data Check Sheet.

Data Check Sheet

Data Collection: 4/2 (Mo/Day/Yr) to 5/18 (Mo/Day/Yr) Area/Dept./Co.: Tinker Town, Inc.

Location: Santa Claus, Ind.

Name(s): Jeff and Linda

Reason/Attribute	Dates/Week Ending							Totals
	4/6	4/13	4/20	4/27	5/4	5/11	5/18	
Incorrect Price	35	28	36	23	40	31	42	235
Wrong Discount	13	18	15	19	14	19	12	110
Incomplete Shipment	0	0	7	10	0	5	0	22
Missed Delivery Date	0	0	0	18	0	0	0	18
Miscellaneous	0	0	0	0	3	0	0	3
Totals	48	46	58	70	57	55	54	388

See pages 144-145 for a larger view of this worksheet.

PLAN

Use the following Data Check Sheet with your team to gather the appropriate data.

Data Check Sheet

Data Collection: ______ to ______ Process Area: ____________
(Mo/Day/Yr) (Mo/Day/Yr)

Location: ____

Name(s): ____

Reason/Attribute	Dates							Totals
Totals								

If people are collecting data that are not part of the PDCA Kaizen team, inform them of the importance of the data being collected and that you will be acting on the data as soon as possible.

Once the data has been collected, organize the data into a Pareto Chart that follows this section.

Pareto Chart

A Pareto Chart is a type of bar chart. Issues are listed in descending order of importance as determined by the Data Check Sheet or other means by which data has been collected. These charts help to prioritize and break down complex problems into smaller chunks. They also help to identify multiple root causes.

A Pareto Chart is based on the proven Pareto principle: 20% of the sources cause 80% of the problem.

Generally, the tallest bars indicate the biggest contributors to the identified problem. Many times before and after improvements are displayed in Pareto Charts to visually convey the applied solution(s).

Approach creating a Pareto Chart as follows:

1. Form a table listing the causes and their frequency as a percentage of the total.
2. Arrange the rows in decreasing order of importance of the causes (i.e. the most important cause first).
3. Add a cumulative percentage column to the table.
4. List the causes on the x-axis and cumulative percentage on the y-axis.
5. Join the above points to form a curve.
6. Plot (on the same graph) a bar graph with causes listed on the x-axis and percent frequency on the y-axis.
7. Draw a line at the 80% mark on the y-axis parallel to the x-axis. Then draw a straight line down to the point of intersection with the curve on the x-axis. This point on the x-axis separates the important causes on the left and less important causes on the right.
8. Continue with the PDCA Kaizen Event methodology.

Case Study for the Pareto Chart - Meeting 1

The team decided to visually convey the Data Check Sheet results on the Pareto Chart. The value of the Pareto Chart is that team members could see instantly the biggest troubled areas. Clearly "Incorrect Price" was first, followed by "Wrong Discount." Combined, they accounted for 88.92% of the returns.

The Problem Definition, Team Charter, and the Pareto Chart were posted on the bulletin board in the cafeteria.

The following is their Pareto Chart.

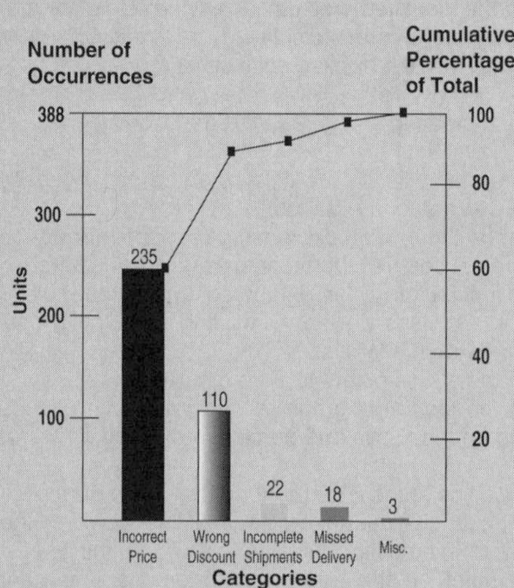

See pages 148-149 for a larger view of this worksheet.

Use the following Pareto outline to plot your data.

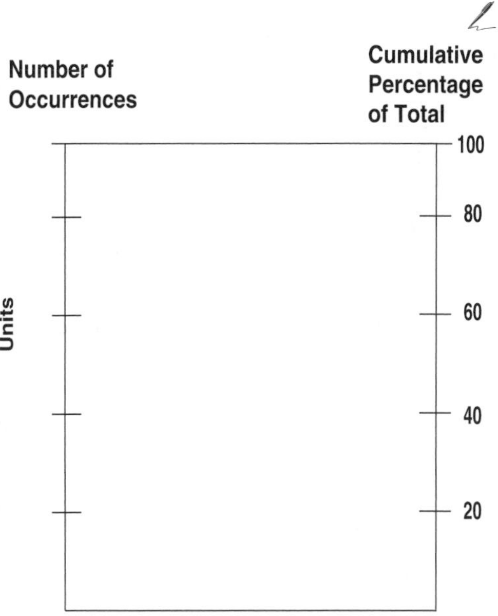

Categories

Note: Measurement Systems Analysis (MSA) can also be used as a data collection methodology. A MSA evaluates the entire process of obtaining measurements to ensure the integrity of data used for analysis and to understand the implications of measurement error for decisions made about a product or process.

Brainstorming

Brainstorming is used to generate a high volume of ideas with team members' full participation. It is free of criticism and judgement. Many of the PDCA Kaizen tools can use Brainstorming to solicit ideas from the team members.

Brainstorming will:

- Encourage open thinking and assure new ideas are presented
- Allow all team members to contribute and thus actively be involved
- Allow ideas from team members to build upon each other

Note: In brainstorming there is one cardinal rule:

No idea is criticized!

There are two basic methods to brainstorm - structured and unstructured.

Structured - A defined method in which each team member contributes his or her ideas in order.

Unstructured - A method in which team members contribute their ideas as they occur (or come to mind).

PLAN

Structured Brainstorming

Structured Brainstorming should be used if:

- The meeting will have a dominant team member
- The unstructured approach was used and numerous team members did not contribute their ideas
- The time element is critical
- The facilitator would possibly be contributing too many of the ideas in an Unstructured Brainstorming method

Approach a Structured Brainstorming session as follows:

1. *Find a quiet room with a flip chart or white board.*

2. *Verbally state the problem, gain a consensus, and write it down so everyone can see it.*

It is critical that everyone understands the issue or problem. The facilitator should get a visual or verbal confirmation from each team member that the problem is understood. Further clarification of the problem at this stage may lend insight into potential solutions. Do not rush this step.

3. *Each team member gives an idea in a round robin fashion.*

Round robin is receiving one idea from each person in a circular manner, until everyone has stated their idea. If a team member does not have an idea for their turn, they can pass. This rotation process encourages full participation. It may also increase some team members' anxieties about having their ideas exposed. The facilitator should acknowledge this and be helpful to any person that seems shy.

4. The team facilitator or scribe writes down each idea.

Each idea should be written large enough for everyone to see. It should be exactly how the person stated the idea, without any interpretation. Confirm with the team member that contributed the idea that what was written, was what they had stated.

5. Collect the ideas until everyone passes, thus indicating all ideas are exhausted.

This process should take between five and fifteen minutes.

6. Review the entire list once everyone has passed.

Remove any ideas that are identical in nature. If there are subtle differences keep them as separate ideas.

7. Show appreciation to everyone for their contributions.

The facilitator should acknowledge that this was very beneficial for the overall team purpose and that it may not have been easy for some.

Unstructured Brainstorming

This method is similar to Structured Brainstorming except ideas are given by anyone at any time. There should be a time limit (again, 15 minutes typically will be more than enough time).

A brainstorming session starts with a clear question and ends with a raw list of ideas. Some will be good and some will not be good. Additional tools and testing will help to determine which of these ideas have the greatest impact on the identified problem.

Case Study for Brainstorming - Meeting 1

The team decided to focus on the Incorrect Price and Wrong Discount. Juan led the team in an unstructured brainstorming session. The whiteboard in the conference room was used to write down all the ideas on possible reasons why there were so many invoicing errors due to the incorrect price and wrong discounts being applied.

The following information is the result of their brainstorming session.

Brainstorming Worksheet

Date: 5/18 Facilitator: Juan

Topic: Why customers have complained that their invoices are not correct.

List below the potential reasons.

- ✔ New fulfillment system not working correctly
- ✔ New bar code readers
- ✔ New sales manager
- ✔ New computers in Shipping
- ✔ Customer Service Representatives not trained
- ✔ New product line of Teddy Bears
- ✔ Customers not using current system correctly
- ✔ Discount schedules not updated regularily
- ✔ Quantity discounts for new products not immediately known
- ✔ Current customer discounts always changing
- ✔ New shipping vendor not connected to system
- ✔ Four retirements
- ✔ Customer Service Representatives entering wrong info
- ✔ Customer Service Representatives overworked
- ✔ Customer Service Representatives not receiving some orders until end of day
- ✔ No avenue for customer order quotes when sales info is not available
- ✔ Customers entering wrong information and Tinker Town accepts as order
- ✔ Supervisors not checking orders
- ✔ Orders over $5000 not following signature process
- ✔ Customers entering wrong discount and new system not verifying it
- ✔ Orders mixed up and customers receiving wrong orders
- ✔ Pick list for customers not accurate
- ✔ New merchant account not transferring order information correctly
- ✔ Part time employee in customer service not trained adequately

See pages 152-153 for a larger view of this worksheet.

Use the following Brainstorming Worksheet to document ideas that are generated in your structured or unstructured brainstorming session.

Brainstorming Worksheet

Date: ______ Facilitator: ____________________

Topic: ____

List below the potential reasons.

✔
✔
✔
✔
✔
✔
✔
✔
✔
✔
✔
✔
✔
✔
✔
✔
✔
✔
✔
✔
✔
✔
✔
✔
✔
✔
✔
✔
✔
✔
✔
✔
✔

Fishbone or Cause and Effect Diagram

A Fishbone Diagram can be used once the problem has been clearly defined. A Fishbone Diagram allows a team to graphically display and explore, in increasing detail, all the possible causes. This will assist in determining the true root cause(s). The problem or effect is identified on the right side of the diagram, and brainstorming and/or other data collection techniques are used to identify and prioritize all possible causes. If done properly and completely, the cause(s) of the problem should be somewhere on the diagram.

Be flexible in the major "bones" or "skeleton" categories that are used. Many times the main categories are Man, Method, Machine (Information Technology), Material, and Mother Nature (Environmental Factors). There is no ideal set of categories or numbers. Make the categories relevant to your problem.

Approach creating a Fishbone Diagram as follows:

1. Write the 4 or 5 main categories on a whitebeard or flip chart as shown in the case study example to follow.
2. Write the effect of the problem as the "head" of the fishbone.
3. List all possible causes of the problem (or effect) in the various 4-5 categories. Use brainstorming techniques to ensure all ideas are explored and documented on the fishbone.
4. Prioritize those causes that need to be investigated further via data collection, beta test, etc. Allow each team member 1-2 votes on the 1 or 2 main causes.
5. Circle the top 1, 2, or 3 items.
6. Continue with the PDCA Kaizen Event methodology.

Case Study for the Fishbone Diagram - Meeting 1

The team organized the ideas from the brainstorming session to further categorize where the problem may lie. The team realized that the Incorrect Price and Wrong Discount were inter-related, however, they wanted to focus only on the Incorrect Price for their first Fishbone.

The following information is the result of their Fishbone Diagram.

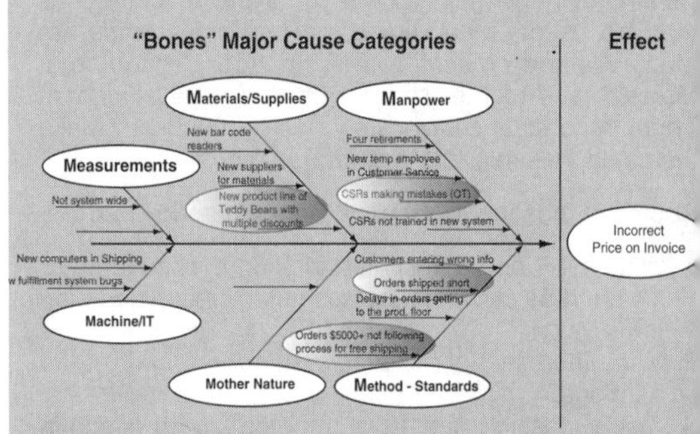

See pages 156-157 for a larger view of this worksheet.

Note: The events from a timeline can also be helpful when creating a Fishbone. A timeline is a visual representation of key events within a particular time period, arranged chronologically.

Use the following Fishbone Diagram with your team to find potential causes to the problem (i.e., effect).

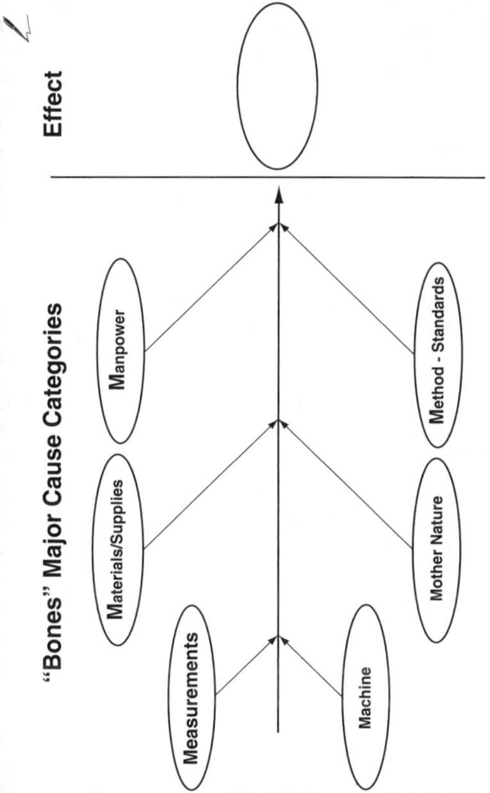

Effect

"Bones" Major Cause Categories

Manpower

Materials/Supplies

Measurements

Method - Standards

Mother Nature

Machine

Once you have completed the Fishbone and circled the most likely causes of the problem use the 5 Why Analysis to further understand the potential problems.

5 Why Analysis

The 5 Why Analysis is a simple problem solving technique that will help a team arrive at the root cause or causes of the problem quickly without statistical analysis. It is closely linked to the Fishbone (Cause and Effect) Diagram. The 5 Why Analysis involves looking at a potential cause of a problem and asking: "Why?" and "What caused this problem?" as many times as it requires to get to the root cause. Very often, the answer to the first "why" will prompt another "why" and the answer to the second "why" will prompt another and so on; hence the name the 5 Whys.

Approach the 5 Why Analysis as follows:

1. List all potential causes of the problem from the Fishbone (top 1-3) and/or Pareto analysis (80% rule).
2. Ask "Why" five times for each potential cause to get to the root cause.
   Note: Asking Why 5 times may or may not be required for each potential cause of the problem; the probable root cause may be identified after only 2 "Why?" questions.
3. Consider if the final "Why" is because of an inadequate standard, not following a standard, or no standard at all. Knowing this will create the need for standard work methods and/or visual controls.
4. Continue with the PDCA Kaizen Event methodology.

Case Study for the 5 Why Analysis - Meeting 2

Based on the Fishbone Diagram, the team did a 5 Why Analysis. Looking at only one column of the 5 Why Analysis, the Tinker Town team discovered that mistakes were being made by the customer service department - Why? 1) Because the Customer Service Representatives (CSRs) had large group of orders in the afternoon - Why? 2) Because International orders were processed at 1:00pm and CSRs could not adapt to any large orders - Why? 3) New system was not updated and CSRs were the only ones trained on the new system - Why? 4) IT was not aware that this was a problem for customer service - Why? 5) IT was not aware this batching of orders and being short-staffed in customer service caused the additional OT. The following information is the result of their 5 Why Analysis.

5 Why Analysis

Problem: Incorrect Prices on Invoices

Cause	Cause	Cause	Cause
CSRs making mistakes (OT)	Orders shipped short	Orders over $5000 not following process	New product line with multiple discounts
Why? Always had large group of orders at the end of the day	**Why?** Not enough inventory to meet demand	**Why?** Orders were not separated	**Why?** Software not configured properly
Why? Intl orders processed at 1:00pm daily and CSRs could not adapt to large orders	**Why?** Production did not have up-to-date inventory levels	**Why?** Sales informed shipping to ship regardless of credit	**Why?** Did not include account special information as well as new customer fields
Why? New system was not updated and only CSRs were trained in new system	**Why?** New fulfillment system only updates bi-weekly	**Why?** Sales knew that new system would cause delays	**Why?** No one was assigned to ensure information would work in new fulfillment system
Why? IT was not aware of Intl orders being processed only at 1:00pm daily	**Why?** Standard feature on new fulfillment system	**Why?** Sales wanted to ensure customer demand be met	**Why?** Four retirements caused workers to absorb as much work as possible
Why? IT did not realize this batching of orders and being short in CS caused addl OT	**Why?**	**Why?**	**Why?**

See pages 160-161 for a larger view of this worksheet.

PLAN

Use the following 5 Why Analysis with your team to find reasons as to what is causing the problem.

5 Why Analysis

Problem: ______________________

Cause	Cause	Cause	Cause
Why?	Why?	Why?	Why?
Why?	Why?	Why?	Why?
Why?	Why?	Why?	Why?
Why?	Why?	Why?	Why?
Why?	Why?	Why?	Why?

Many times the 5 Why Analysis and Fishbone Diagram will raise questions as to how a process is running. If that is the case, then map the process by using the process mapping methodology (that follows) or conduct a value stream mapping session.

Flowcharts

Creating a flowchart or process map allows for a visual representation of a sequence of activities or tasks consisting of people, work duties, and transactions that occur for the delivery of a product or service. This will help the PDCA Kaizen team gain a consensus of exactly what is happening in the process.

Flowcharts use standard symbols to represent a type of operation, process, and/or set of tasks to be performed. The use of standardized symbols provides a common language for the Kaizen team to visualize problems and also makes flowcharts easier to read and understand, and makes them a viable source to see areas of waste or process variation.

There are five types of flowcharts: basic, process, deployment, opportunity, and spaghetti diagram.

1. Basic flowcharts (macro level) identify all the major steps in a process - usually no more than six steps. They are mostly used for the 30,000 foot view for management review.

2. Process flowcharts (micro level) examine the process in detail. They will provide a detailed visual listing of all the major and sub-steps in a process. This is the ground level listing of the tasks and activities.

3. Deployment flowcharts are similar to process flowcharts but they also visually convey the people (or departments) who are involved in the process. These flowcharts are helpful if the process being mapped crosses departmental boundaries.

4. Opportunity flowcharts are a variation of the process flowchart, but differentiates between value-added and non value-added activities.

5. Spaghetti diagram flowcharts use a continuous line to trace the path of a part, document, person, or service that is being provided through all its phases. Spaghetti diagrams expose inefficient layouts and large distances traveled between steps. These diagrams should also display electronic information flow (e-mails, spreadsheets, documents, etc.).

Use the following flowchart symbols to map your current process flow.

Ovals are used to represent beginning and ending points of the process.

Rectangles are used to describe an action taken or a task completed.

Diamonds contain questions that require a "Yes" or "No" decision and indicate appropriate process flow.

A Document is used to represent a paper document produced during the process.

Multi-Page Documents are used to represent a report or an output with multiple pages.

A modified rectangle represents a standard to follow (i.e., protocol, standard of service, standard operating procedure, governmental regulation, etc.).

An arrow represents the direction of the process flow.

A queue symbol represents a delay in the process.

A circle is used to show that the flow continues on a different page or to another process.

Note: This is the standard set of flowchart icons. The team can create news ones if that would assist in improving the visualization of the process flow.

The following are examples of each type of flowchart for a medical office visit, something we are all familiar with, as well as the basic steps to follow. *The last flowchart will denote the case study process flowchart.*

Basic flowchart (macro level)

Approach creating this flowchart as follows:

1. Define the process boundaries with the beginning and ending points of the process.
2. Create no more than six boxes denoting what is occurring between the start and end points.
3. Review the flowchart with management to ensure everyone is on the same page with this macro view of the process or work flow.
4. Continue with more detailed flowcharting or value stream mapping (if appropriate) and follow the PDCA Kaizen Event methodology.

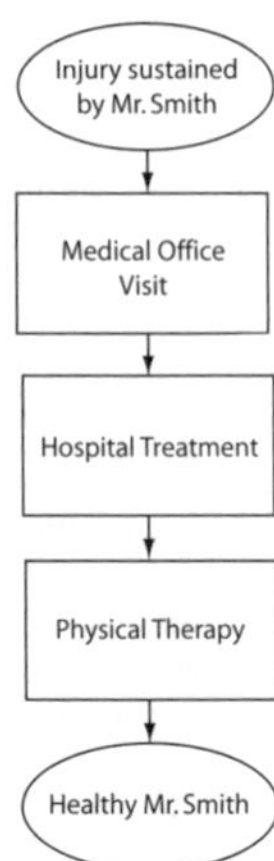

Deployment flowchart

Approach creating this flowchart as follows:

1. Identify the right people needed to develop the flowchart.
2. Define the process boundaries with the beginning and ending points of the process.
3. List the major steps (or time element) of the process vertically on the left sheet of paper.
4. List the responsible department (or process worker) across the top, each in a separate column.
5. List all the steps in their appropriate column and ensure they are connected by arrows.
6. Circulate the flowchart to other people within the process for input and/or clarification (if appropriate).
7. Identify areas for improvement.
8. Create the new flowchart and continue with the PDCA Kaizen Event methodology.

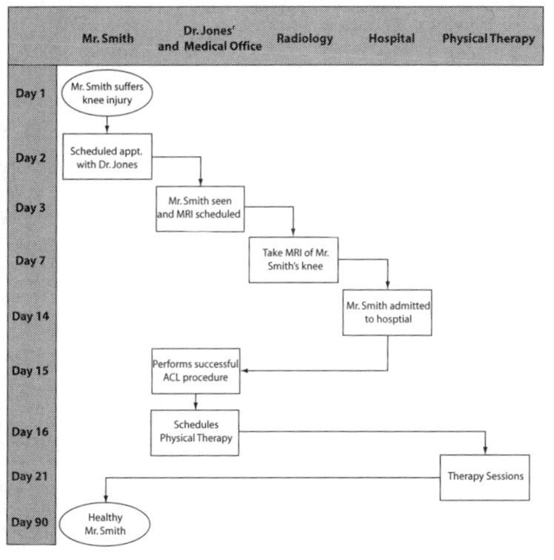

Opportunity flowchart

Approach creating this flowchart as follows:

1. Create a process flowchart (micro level).
2. Create separate columns on a flip chart or whitebeard. Label one Value-Added and the other one Non Value-Added (or Cost-Added Only).
3. List each step from the process flowchart in either column and ensure they are connected by arrows. Expand the steps to show specific areas of concern, if needed.
4. Identify areas for improvement.
5. Create the new flowchart and continue with the PDCA Kaizen Event methodology.

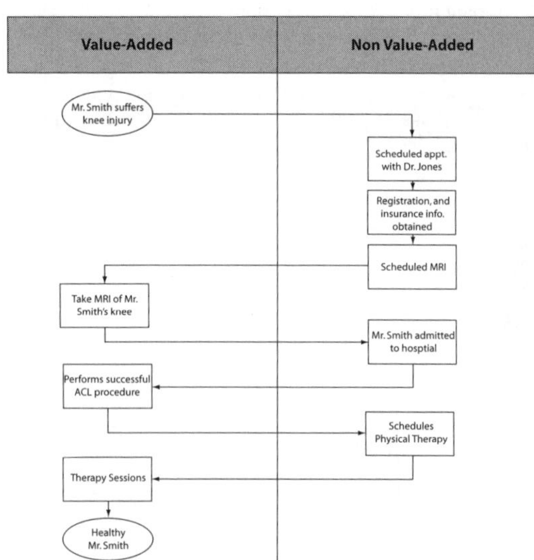

Spaghetti diagram flowchart

Approach creating this flowchart as follows:

1. Define the beginning and ending of the process.
2. Obtain an engineering drawing or create a scale representation of the physical layout of the process.
3. List each step of the process on the flowchart (or on a separate piece of paper).
4. Label and draw each of the steps (3) sequentially as how the process flows. Connect each step with an arrow line denoting the flow.
5. Gain a consensus if the process is inefficient (i.e., too many touches, too many hand-offs, too much travel, etc.).
6. Identify areas for improvement.
7. Create the new flowchart and continue with the PDCA Kaizen Event methodology.

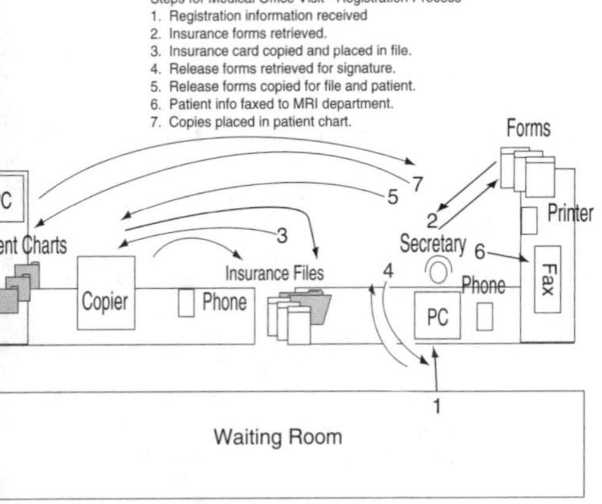
Steps for Medical Office Visit - Registration Process
1. Registration information received
2. Insurance forms retrieved.
3. Insurance card copied and placed in file.
4. Release forms retrieved for signature.
5. Release forms copied for file and patient.
6. Patient info faxed to MRI department.
7. Copies placed in patient chart.
Forms
Printer
Secretary
Fax
Phone
PC
Insurance Files
Phone
Copier
Charts
Waiting Room
1
2
3
4
5
6
7

Process flowchart (micro level)

Approach creating this flowchart as follows:

1. Identify the right people needed to develop the flowchart. This may require people from outside the PDCA Kaizen Team for their expertise and knowledge.
2. Define the process boundaries with the beginning and ending points of the process.
3. Define the level of detail required.
4. Determine conditions and boundaries for the process flow.
5. List all the steps contained within the process flow. The Kaizen Event team may need to walk the process.
6. Circulate the flowchart to other people within the process for input and/or clarification.
7. Identify areas for improvement.
8. Create the new flowchart and continue with the PDCA Kaizen Event methodology.

Case Study for the Process Flowchart - Meeting 2

In reviewing the data so far, the team members began finger-pointing and blaming other departments until Kate spoke up.

"Stop it. This is NOT about people, it's about process."

"Just what's that supposed to mean?" Susan from Customer Service asked. "When customers call about their invoice mistakes, I'm the one who takes the heat."

"I understand that," Kate said. "That can be tough. However, correcting the problem isn't going to be accomplished by attacking people. We'll do a process flowchart and get a better understanding of what's actually happening in the customer ordering process."

"So, if everyone agrees, let's process map the ordering system for Teddy Bears that would include new customer orders to get a handle on how it currently operates." Juan summarized.

The following information is the result of their process map.

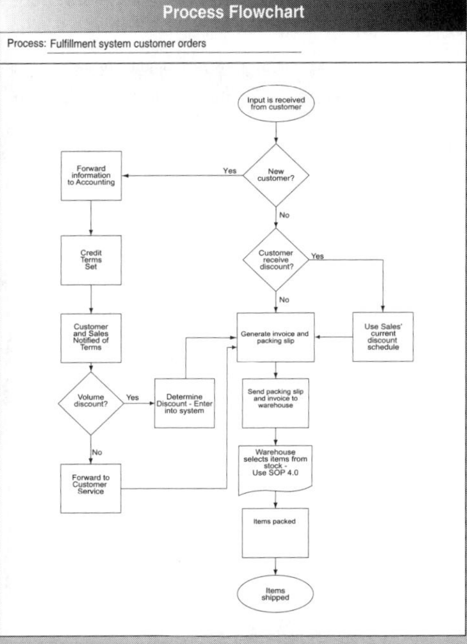

See pages 164-165 for a larger view of this worksheet.

As you continue with the PDCA Kaizen Event methodology, flowcharts can be used with additional tools in the identification of bottlenecks, delays, weak links, poorly defined steps, and cost-only steps. By creating a flowchart, everyone can gain a consensus on how the process is currently running and be in a better position to contribute ideas for improvements.

Use the following Flowchart Worksheet with your team to document process flow.

Flowchart Worksheet

Use the following standard symbols to represent the process flow.

Start or end of process	Document	Direction of process flow
Task or activity	Multiple documents	Delay, queue time
Decisions - branches	Standard or protocol	Connector

PLAN Readiness Guide

P D C A

The questions listed below should be reviewed with the team to ensure all appropriate tools are completed (if appropriate) prior to implementing the next phase. A majority of the questions should be answered with a Yes.

PLAN

Readiness Guide for PLAN

If you answer No to more than half of these, then consider using additional tools in the PLAN phase.

1. Do meetings have an agenda, timekeeper, and scribe? ❒Yes ❒No
2. Has a Team Charter been created and a Team Champion assigned? ❒Yes ❒No
3. Has the problem been clearly defined? ❒Yes ❒No
4. Is brainstorming being used effectively so everyone is involved? ❒Yes ❒No
5. Has enough data been collected on the problem? ❒Yes ❒No
6. Has a Pareto Chart been created displaying appropriate data? ❒Yes ❒No
7. Has a 5 Why Analysis been performed? ❒Yes ❒No
8. Has a Fishbone Diagram been created? ❒Yes ❒No
9. Has an appropriate flowchart been created? ❒Yes ❒No
10. Does everyone understand the four stages of team development? ❒Yes ❒No
11. Has the customer been identified and quantified (takt time)? ❒Yes ❒No
12. Will the improvements planned help stabilize the process(es)? ❒Yes ❒No
13. Will flow between people, material, and/or data be improved? ❒Yes ❒No
14. Will people, material, and/or data access become more efficient? ❒Yes ❒No
15. Does everyone understand waste? ❒Yes ❒No
16. Has an A3 Report or Storyboard been started? ❒Yes ❒No

Case Study for Lean Considerations

Kate knew that more needed to be done for improvements beyond the 90% customer survey satisfaction level. She considered the following additional Lean tools to be used:

5S - Organizing the customer service department because all CSRs had their own filing system for customer orders and quotes, also, in manufacturing, it was apparent that aisleways were not marked, workers were not consistent in placement of their tools - people were always looking for something - and that equated to waste of travel, motion, etc.
Standard Work - Sales had many different methods in which to give customers large discounts and that information could not be entered into the new fulfillment system in a timely manner
Continuous flow - The new fulfillment system did not accommodate real time international orders due to the merchant account system of PayPal, so information was not Just-In-Time
Visual controls - The Customer Service Manager had no idea until 3:00 - 4:00pm each day that the department had to work overtime
Work Load Balancing - It was apparent, as Kate walked through the sales and customer service departments, that everyone may not be as busy as they could be, and that some work load balancing could be of value
Value stream mapping - A vision or road map to establish a priority system to work on all these areas
Mistake Proofing - To ensure customer discount and pricing information cannot be entered incorrectly

Kate reflected, "WOW, how can we be in business with all of these other problem areas?" Kate knew she was in it for the long term and needed others at the company to more fully understand Lean. She arranged for Rita and Juan to attend a Lean seminar at the local college and suggested they schedule a Lean benchmarking trip for the team.

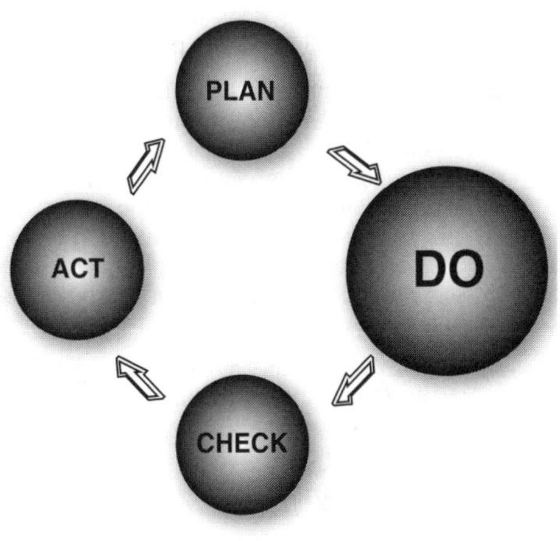
PLAN
ACT
DO
CHECK

DO - *develop and implement a solution(s).*

The DO stage of the PDCA process involves testing (i.e., prototyping, small scale experimenting) many of the Interim Containment Actions, as well as any Permanent Countermeasures. Interim Containment Actions may or may not turn into Permanent Countermeasures. Interim Containment Actions are temporary fixes or "band-aids" to fix the problem. Whatever is done in this stage should minimize the risk of disrupting regular processing.

Throughout this stage, employees may experience a significant change to a newer way of doing things (a new standard, an update to an existing standard, etc.). This change may or may not be agreeable, acceptable, or easy to do. Most likely, the process(es) that has to be changed or updated has been that way for many years. In order to make the implementation of any type of change occur smoothly, it is important that the team understands how resistance to this change may occur.

This phase will also require a detailed Training Plan to ensure the Interim Containment Actions, as well as any Permanent Countermeasures, are fully understood prior to the testing or prototyping.

In the DO Phase, the following tools will be defined:

- ✔ Accepting Change
- ✔ Countermeasure Kaizen Log
- ✔ Failure Prevention Analysis (Mistake Proofing)
- ✔ Training Plan
- ✔ Gantt Chart

Note: These are the basic tools that can be used in the DO Phase, however, they can also be used in the PLAN, CHECK, and ACT Phases as well.

Accepting Change

Understanding the resistance to change will allow for clearer communications. Change is inevitable. ***Most resistance to change is due to the lack of communication***.

Approach resistance to change as follows:

1. Understand the 4 S's of resistance.

Resistance to Skills is due to the increase in anxiety of new work requirements that may appear too technical, too complicated, or require skills that a staff member may not have. The easiest and most effective way to address this fear is to provide employees with information, training, and education. This will prepare them to master the skills required to implement the changes. Lean requires a different, more efficient way of doing things.

Resistance to Support is due to people feeling that as new processes are streamlined, their jobs may be at risk. In some cases, this may be a justifiable fear. Some job functions will change and some departments will be consolidated. But as facilities deploy the Lean tools, they will be in a better position for growth and will then have the ability to shift people to other functions. Acknowledge the difficulty this presents to the employee. Empathize with the employees' concern of the changes that may affect them. Point out the benefits of Lean as a long term solution for job security, job satisfaction, and corporate viability.

Resistance to Society is due to some people being resistant to *any* ideas that do not originate with them. Fortunately, implementing Lean tools and practices is a team effort. There are many opportunities for everyone to provide input into how these new systems and procedures are developed and deployed.

Resistance to Stress is due to the variety of difficult challenges the staff may be facing, not only in the office, but in their personal lives as well. If an employee is not making the transition well, the manager/supervisor should quickly find out what the problem is. It may be related to outside stresses not controlled by the organization. In these situations, it is important to understand the personal situation affecting the work. Create realistic expectations for the acceptance to the proposed changes.

2. Analyze quick "adapters."

Recognize employees who are the informal leaders. They are present in any workplace. Managers and supervisors must be on the lookout for these leaders. When they are identified, utilize their skills wisely. Remember, no change can be effective and sustained without employees who have the vision, desire, and willingness to see it through.

There are five levels of support (or lack of) usually found within an organization going through change. They are:

- People who will make it happen
- People who will help it happen
- People who will let it happen
- People who are mildly against it
- People who will actively sabotage it

3. Apply the 80/20 rule.

Usually no more than 20% of the employees will fall into the last two categories. Of that 20%, 80% of those people can be converted into supporters, while 20% may never accept any change. Mathematically, 0.8 + (0.8 x 0.2) = 0.96, or 96% will be in support. Focus on the 96%!

4. Conduct a meeting.

Conduct a meeting with your group of employees to address the changes and any fears they may have. Also, since information has been posted, data collected, and process maps shared, ask for additional ideas about the improvement initiative. Finally, explain any training that needs to occur.

5. Continue with the PDCA Kaizen Event methodology.

Key Points for Resistance to Change

- Continue to assure employees of the organization's need to improve. The benefits of a profitable organization will position it for growth while providing job security.
- Continually look for ways to communicate the change process (i.e., company newsletters, website, luncheon meetings, etc.).
- Find those informal, day-to-day champions, and utilize them wisely.
- Ensure reward and recognition are used for team and individual contributions.
- Create visual aids about the changes well in advance (i.e., posters, notices, storyboards, etc.).
- Prior to any changes, educate everyone impacted by the proposed changes.

Use the following Managing Change Checklist to assist your team in this process.

Managing Change Checklist

Directions:

1. Spend only a few minutes reviewing this checklist.
2. Use the checklist with the PDCA Kaizen team prior to rolling out any changes.
3. Focus on the weak spots that have scores less than 3.

Rating System: 1 is the lowest score (Poor) and 5 is the highest (Excellent) Poor 1 2 3 4 5 Excellent	Score
1. Is there a clear and compelling reason for adopting this improvement?	
2. Is objective data available to convince any skeptics?	
3. Do people feel the urgency for this change?	
4. Are the motivators known for each person affected by the change?	
5. Does the senior executive team support this change?	
6. Has the proposed change been communicated to all stakeholders?	
7. Are the right people selected for the right roles?	
8. Are performance measurements and reporting systems made visual for the change?	
9. Is the training plan adequately resourced?	
10. Are project management principles and methods being used (i.e., Team Charter, Agendas, Timelines, etc.)?	
11. Is support in place, ensuring transfer of training to the workplace (i.e., standards of work)?	
12. Are successes celebrated?	
13. Have I (we) studied the changes carefully and identified if anyone is likely to lose something -- including what I (we) may be likely to lose?	
14. What actions can I (we) take to help people deal more successfully with the changes that are taking place with this PDCA Kaizen Event? What can I (we) do today to get started on this aspect of the change?	
TOTAL:	

Countermeasures - Interim and Permanent

Countermeasures are the short and long term actions taken by the team members to isolate and eliminate the root cause(s) of the problem.

Interim Containment Actions are those activities that will immediately isolate the problem from your customer. This may require additional resources, manpower, etc. and many times is considered a band-aid until Permanent Countermeasures can be put in place. Interim Containment Actions may become Permanent Countermeasures if proven successful and cost effective.

Permanent Countermeasures are those activities that modify or create a new standard. These changes will ensure that the root cause(s) of the problem will not occur under similar circumstances.

Permanent Countermeasures may not be completed at the same time that the Interim Containment Actions are decided. This would be due to the additional data analysis that would be obtained from the Interim Containment Actions.

Approach creating Interim Containment Actions and Permanent Countermeasures as follows:

1. Gain a consensus on the exact activities that are required for the improvement.
2. Determine appropriate resources for each action.
3. Determine the start date, who will be responsible, and due date for the action to be done. Also, denote any measurements or targets to be reached.
4. Determine, initially, if the action is a temporary fix or is part of a longer term solution. Note it as such.
5. Continue with the PDCA Kaizen Event methodology.

Case Study for the Countermeasure Kaizen Log Meeting 2

Once the team discovered the problems, decisions had to be made as to what steps to take. This involved the following two types of countermeasures:

1. Interim Containment Actions that had to be immediately implemented to stop the incorrect invoices from occurring
2. Permanent Countermeasures to eliminate the root cause(s) of the problem, as well as the implementation of Lean tools to create a system of continuous improvement, had to be planned, tested, and implemented

Kate believed this was a good time to start the team thinking Lean and said, "It may take us a bit longer to learn some of these Lean tools but I believe it will be good for Tinker Town in the long term."

The team agreed. They subsequently reviewed all the tools used to date and came up with the following Interim Containment Actions and Permanent Countermeasures.

The following is their Countermeasure Kaizen Log.

Countermeasures Kaizen Log

Problem: Customer Survey negative trend due to 8% of all invoices incorrect **Date:** 5/22

Causes	Interim Containment Actions	WHO	START DATE	END DATE
1. New product line w/ mult. discounts	a. Create manual system w/ Sales	B.K.	5/22	6/28
2. CSRs making mistakes (OT)	b. Assign data input to those trained	W.B.	5/22	6/15
3. Orders shipped short	c. Supervisors to check all orders and invoices	D.T.	5/22	6/24
4. Orders over $5000+ not following process	d. Create red folder for orders over $5000 and include checklist before shipping	J.B.	5/22	6/24
	Permanent Countermeasures	**WHO**	**START DATE**	**END DATE**
1. New product line w/ mult. discounts	a. Update new fulfillment system	J.I.	6/1	6/30
	b. Create new Sales update program	K.W.	5/22	6/22
	c. Create Mistake Proofing IT solution for product discounts	J.B.	5/30	6/15
2. CSRs making mistakes (OT)	a. Create training plan for all CSRs and implement	W.B.	6/1	6/8
	b. Determine takt time and pitch for customer orders	B.K.	5/30	6/4
	c. Create standard work and balance work loads	B.K.	5/30	6/15
3. Orders shipped short	a. Create Standard Work Chart and post	R.H.	6/15	6/30
	b. Update fulfillment system to verify order and price disc.	J.I.	6/1	6/15
4. Orders over $5000+ not following process	a. Create a visual control on-line checklist and train everyone	J.I.	6/1	6/15
	b. Value stream map the process for further analysis	K.W.	6/15	6/30

See pages 170-171 for a larger view of this worksheet.

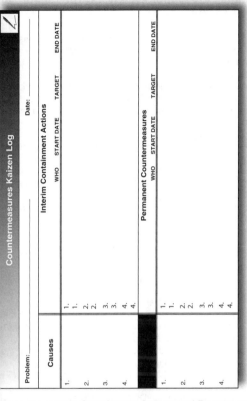

Countermeasures Kaizen Log

Problem: ______ Date: ______

Causes	Interim Containment Actions WHO START DATE TARGET END DATE
1.	1. 1.
2.	2. 2.
3.	3. 3.
4.	4. 4.
	Permanent Countermeasures WHO START DATE TARGET END DATE
1.	1. 1.
2.	2. 2.
3.	3. 3.
4.	4. 4.

DO

Once the Interim Containment Actions and Permanent Countermeasures have been decided, the team should brainstorm to identify any potential problems that may arise.

Failure Prevention Analysis (precursor to Mistake Proofing)

Failure Prevention Analysis is a technique that allows the Kaizen Team to anticipate potential problems in the solution before implementing it. This allows the team to be proactive to prevent the solution(s) from going wrong. A Lean tool known as poka-yoke would be the procedures, visual controls, alarm notifications, etc. that prevent a mistake from being made or to ensure the mistake, if made, is obvious at a glance.

Poka-yoke is Japanese for mistake proofing. It is derived from "poka" - inadvertent mistake and "yoke" - avoid. The cause of a defect from a process is the result of process error. This analysis, and the subsequent planning, (i.e., of using mistake proofing devices), will contribute to the sustainability of the PDCA Kaizen Event solution(s). Many times visual controls will play a large role in reducing the opportunity for errors.

Approach conducting a Failure Prevention Analysis as follows:

1. Create a list of potential failures for each Action and Countermeasure (if applicable).
2. Rank the potential failures by designating the potential and consequence of each going wrong on a scale from 1 to 10 through a team consensus.
3. Multiply the potential and consequence for each of the potential failures (1) to give overall rating.
4. Rank each potential failure from highest to lowest (1 - XX).
5. Brainstorm with the PDCA Kaizen Event team to modify any Actions and/or Countermeasures to lessen the likelihood of the solution causing a problem.
6. Continue with the PDCA Kaizen Event methodology.

Case Study for the Failure Prevention Analysis Worksheet - Meeting 2

Kate explained the concept of mistake proofing and wanted to make sure that any Interim Containment Action or Permanent Countermeasure that were planned were not going to affect the customer or another process adversely.

The following is their Failure Prevent Analysis Worksheet.

Failure Prevention Analysis Worksheet

Directions:

1. List all potential failures.
2. Assign a number from 1 to 10 for the potential and consequence of an activity going wrong.
3. Multiply the potential and consequence and rank from highest to lowest.

No chance for error or no consequence — High chance of error and great consequence

1 2 3 4 5 6 7 8 9 10

Potential Failure	Potential	Consequence	Overall Rating	Ranking
A. Create manual system w/ Sales	4	8	32	4
B. Assign data input to only those trained	3	7	21	2
C. Supervisors to check all orders and invoices	7	9	63	6
D. Create red folder for orders over $5000 and include checklist	6	9	54	5
E. Update new fulfillment system	2	9	18	1
F. Create new Sales update program	3	9	27	3
G.				
H.				
I.				

Please provide any other comments or suggestions for improvements.

The team decided to have the supervisors assign a back-up person to assist them in checking all orders. It was acknowledged that due to the retirements they have been exceptionally busy.

See pages 174-175 for a larger view of this worksheet.

DO

Use the following worksheet to conduct your preventior analysis brainstorming and planning session.

Failure Prevention Analysis Worksheet

Directions:

1. List all potential failures.
2. Assign a number from 1 to 10 for the potential and consequence of an activity going wrong.
3. Multiply the potential and consequence and rank from highest to lowest.

No chance for error or no consequence								High chance of error and great consequence	
1	2	3	4	5	6	7	8	9	10

Potential Failure	Potential	Consequence	Overall Rating	Ranking
A.				
B.				
C.				
D.				
E.				
F.				
G.				
H.				
I.				

Please provide any other comments or suggestions for improvements.

Training Plan

A training plan is required to ensure everyone understands and follows the new process(es) derived from the Interim Containment Actions and/or Permanent Countermeasures. The training should be:

- ✔ Easy to understand
- ✔ Visually effective
- ✔ Timely and thorough
- ✔ Sufficient in length for questions and practice (if applicable)
- ✔ Verifiable to ensure it is effective
- ✔ Multi-lingual (if appropriate)

People rapidly forget the information from any type of formal training unless they begin to use it right away. After two weeks, most people retain about 30% of any learning that was associated with the training. Therefore, it is important to conduct the training immediately before anyone is required to adhere to the new process change. The training should include as many visual aids as practical which will greatly assist it to "stick" in the minds of the employees. The visuals should be included in the final standard work procedures, as well as other Lean tools that would be appropriate (i.e., visual controls, mistake proofing, etc.).

Approach creating a training plan as follows:

1. Ensure the new process has been proven effective and is well documented (consider different languages if appropriate).
2. Create standard work procedures that are visual.
3. Create a system for improving the standards.
4. Create a training matrix to ensure everyone is training to the standard.
5. Continue with the PDCA Kaizen Event methodology.

DO

Case Study for the Training Plan - Meeting 2

Juan took the lead in coordinating the training. He, along with Rita, recently attended the Lean seminar at the local college. He decided that standard work tools could be of value in the development and delivery of any training. He believed that if the solutions to any of the problems were related to training, then if it was done correctly, with the proper visual controls, then it could be short and to-the-point. Juan's vision was to have Standard Work Charts (i.e., a visual indicating the sequence of each process step) posted in each CSR area for the new fulfillment system, as well as who had been trained in the process.

The following is their Training Plan Worksheet.

Training Plan Worksheet

Problem: Customer Survey negative trend due to 8% of all invoices incorrect **Date:** 5/30

Causes	INTERIM CONTAINMENT ACTIONS/ PERMANENT COUNTERMEASURES	TRAINEE(S)	TRAINER	MATERIALS REQUIRED	START DATE	LOCATION
1. New product line w/ mult. discounts	1. Create manual system w/ Sales	Mkt, Sales,CS	B.K.	Excel	5/24	Sales Conf. Rm
3. Orders shipped short	3. Supervisors to check all orders and invoices	Sups.	D.T.	Visual Aid	5/26	Sales Conf. Rm
4. Orders over $5000+ not following process	4. Create red folder for orders over $5000 and include checklist	Sups./ Shipping	J.B.	Folders/ Labels	5/26	Training Room
1. New product line w/ mult. discounts	1. Update new fulfillment system 1. Create new Sales update program 1. Create Mistake Proofing IT solution	Mkt, Sales,CS	K.W.	Screen Printouts	6/15	Sales Conf. Rm
3. Orders shipped short	3. Create Standard Work Chart and post 3. Update fulfillment system.	CS/ Shipping	J.J.	Stand. Wrk.Chart	6/15	Training Room

See pages 178-179 for a larger view of this worksheet.

Use the following Training Plan Worksheet to organize, schedule, and plan the training required to support the implementation of the Interim Containment Actions and Permanent Countermeasures from your Kaizen Event.

Training Plan Worksheet

Problem: ____________________ Date: ____________

Causes	IMMEDIATE CONTAINMENT ACTIONS/ PERMANENT COUNTERMEASURES	TRAINEE(S)	TRAINER	MATERIALS REQUIRED	START DATE	LOCATION

DO

Gantt Chart

A Gantt Chart consists of a table of project task information and a bar chart that graphically displays Interim Containment Actions and Permanent Countermeasures scheduled tasks, while depicting progress in relation to time. It is similar in nature to a timeline that denotes actions over time. Gantt Charts should be updated regularly.

Note: Microsoft Project and Visio have effective Gantt Chart programs.

Approach creating a Gantt Chart as follows:

1. List all the steps that need to be completed that would comprise the Interim Containment Actions and Permanent Countermeasures.
2. Organize listed tasks in sequential order.
3. Assign a person or a group of people to be responsible for each step.
4. Decide how long each step will take, when it can be started in relation to the other steps, and when it should be completed (or in place until Permanent Countermeasures are implemented).
5. Develop a horizontal bar chart to portray the above steps. Include sequencing and overlapping of the steps as needed.
6. Document assumptions and develop contingency plans to implement in case some of the assumptions proved wrong or a task needed modification. For example, if a step requires four weeks to implement and it must be completed prior to another step, detail the contingency plan to ensure that the next step would not be delayed.
7. Continue with the PDCA Kaizen Event methodology

Case Study for the Gantt Chart - Meeting 2

Having plans without timetables makes no sense, so the team used a Gantt Chart to establish time tables for implementing the actions from the Countermeasure Kaizen Log.

The following information is their Gantt Chart.

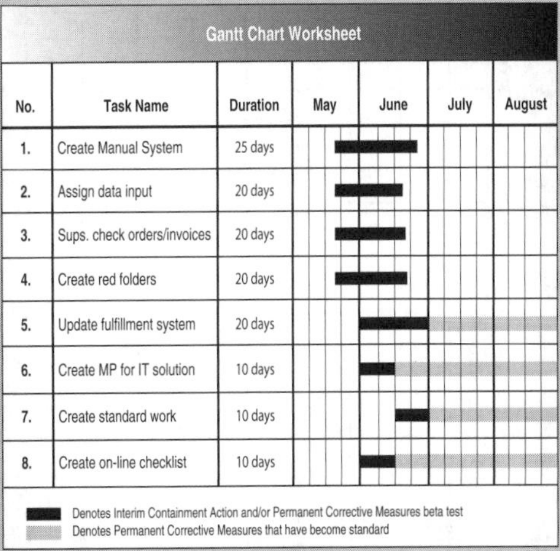

Gantt Chart Worksheet

No.	Task Name	Duration	May	June	July	August
1.	Create Manual System	25 days				
2.	Assign data input	20 days				
3.	Sups. check orders/invoices	20 days				
4.	Create red folders	20 days				
5.	Update fulfillment system	20 days				
6.	Create MP for IT solution	10 days				
7.	Create standard work	10 days				
8.	Create on-line checklist	10 days				

Denotes Interim Containment Action and/or Permanent Corrective Measures beta test

Denotes Permanent Corrective Measures that have become standard

See pages 182-183 for a larger view of this worksheet.

DO

Use the following Gantt Chart worksheet with your team to organize and plan the activities required for effective implementation of the Interim Containment Actions and Permanent Countermeasures.

Gantt Chart Worksheet

No.	Task Name	Duration	Time Interval (Days/Weeks/Months)			
1.						
2.						
3.						
4.						
5.						
6.						
7.						
8.						

DO Readiness Guide

The questions listed below should be reviewed with the team to ensure all appropriate tools are completed (if appropriate) prior to implementing the next phase. A majority of the questions should be answered with a Yes.

Readiness Guide for DO

If you answer No to more than half of these, then consider using additional tools in the DO phase.

1. Does everyone understand the need for change?	❐Yes	❐No
2. Has the PLAN been thoroughly communicated to all involved?	❐Yes	❐No
3. Have Interim Containment Actions been taken?	❐Yes	❐No
4. Is data being collected to verify the success of any/all changes?	❐Yes	❐No
5. Has a Countermeasures Kaizen Log been created?	❐Yes	❐No
6. Is everyone completing their assigned tasks on time?	❐Yes	❐No
7. Has a Failure Prevention Analysis been completed?	❐Yes	❐No
8. Has a training plan been completed?	❐Yes	❐No
9. Has a Gantt Chart been created?	❐Yes	❐No
10. Are standard methods being implemented and documented?	❐Yes	❐No
11. Is there a plan to ensure customers are not adversely impacted?	❐Yes	❐No
12. Is data being made visible (if appropriate)?	❐Yes	❐No
13. Are visual aids being used to identify problems if they occur?	❐Yes	❐No
14. Are meetings effective?	❐Yes	❐No
15. Has the A3 Report or Storyboard been updated?	❐Yes	❐No

Case Study for Lean Considerations

Kate had felt the team had been progressing very well. It was an aggressive schedule to implement all the Interim Containment Actions as well as Permanent Countermeasures in the six weeks.

Kate, Juan, and Rita had met to discuss the opportunities this problem had brought to Tinker Town, Inc., in that, Lean was a business improvement philosophy, as well as a set of tools for an organization.

Kate said to Rita and Juan, "I like how both of you are starting to use some Lean terminology. For example, in the Permanent Countermeasures you both used the words of takt time, visual control, standard work, and some others, which I thought was excellent. Keep it up. I believe the first part of any Lean training is just simple communication. It is common sense, but Lean allows people to communicate some common sense approaches in a standard way."

Rita agreed and stated, "Yes, Kate, you are right. It has taken me some time since this first problem came to our attention that we can use some of these Lean practices not only correct the current problem, but put in place a better process for our customers. I also know that everyone on the team - so far - is onboard."

Kate thanked Rita and Juan for their support.

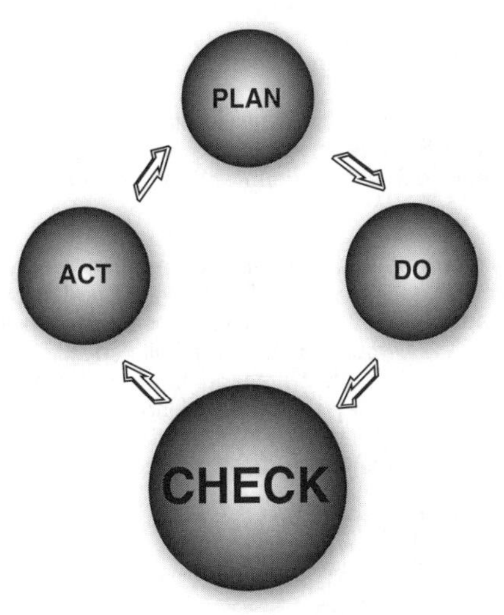
PLAN
DO
CHECK
ACT

CHECK - to verify results.

The CHECK stage of the PDCA process involves confirming or establishing a means of monitoring the solution(s). Some of the following questions will need to be addressed:

Is the solution having the expected effect?
Are there any unexpected problems?
Is the solution or solutions appropriate to implement system wide?
Are the correct measurements in place to correlate the changes (i.e., Interim Containment Actions and/or Permanent Countermeasures) with the problem that was first identified?

Usually problems and their impact are measured by certain metrics (decided in the PLAN phase and/or by the Team Charter). This phase involves measuring results in the DO phase versus benchmark results specified in the PLAN phase. In project management terminology, this means evaluating key performance indicators in light of beta tests (prototyping, etc.) in a practical setting prior to wide-scale implementation.

In the CHECK Phase, the following tools will be defined:

- ✔ Impact Maps
- ✔ Run Charts

Note: These are the basic tools that can be used in the CHECK Phase, however, they can also be used in the PLAN, DO, and ACT Phases as well.

Impact Map

The Impact Map is a method by which a team can identify the solutions that will most likely have the greatest impact on the problem with the least effort.

The team should reach a consensus on the EASE of implementation, as well as the IMPACT that it will have on the result.

Approach creating an Impact Map as follows:

1. Utilize the appropriate Interim Containment Actions and/or Permanent Countermeasures.
2. Create a graph with the vertical-axis denoting IMPACT; 0 being at the bottom (label as LOW) and 10 at the top (label as HIGH). Create the horizontal axis denoting EASE with the left being 1 (label as VERY DIFFICULT) and the far right being 10 (label as VERY EASY).
3. Create appropriate numbers 1-10 for each axis.
4. Divide the graph into four quadrants.
5. Brainstorm with the team and assign each item listed in (1) to an area of the map.
6. Determine which items will have the greatest impact with the least amount of effort. Consider these (and any others that would be practical to implement) as Permanent Countermeasures and have the team prepare for wide-scale implementation.
7. Communicate to management those items that would be very difficult and may have a high impact, but may be beyond the scope of this particular PDCA Kaizen Event.
8. Continue with the PDCA Kaizen Event methodology.

Case Study for the Impact Map - Meeting 2

The team decided to place most of the Permanen[t] Countermeasures on an Impact Map. This helped them to determine the amount of time and resources that may be required.

The following information is their Impact Map Worksheet

Impact Map Worksheet			
IMPACT of the result (1 - Very Low to 10 - Very High) EASE of achieving (1 - Very Difficult to 10 - Very Easy)			
No.	Ideas/Actions/Countermeasures	EASE	IMPACT
1.	Update new fulfillment system	2	9
2.	Create new Sales update program	3	6
3	Create IT solutions for discounts	2	10
4.	Create training plan for CSRs	10	3
5.	Create standard work and balance work loads	8	8
6.	Update fulfillment system to verify order and price discounts	7	9
7.	Create visual control for on-line checklist and train everyone	9	7

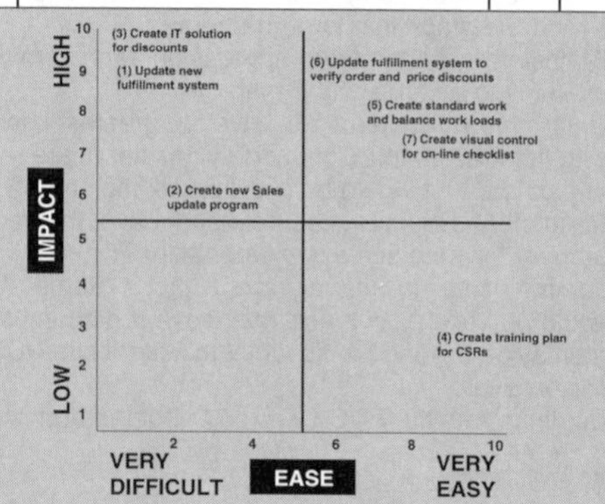

See pages 186-187 for a larger view of this worksheet.

Use the following Impact Map Worksheet to assist your team in identifying the easier solutions to implement from the more difficult and time consuming ones. This will also assist in determining resource allocations.

Impact Map Worksheet

IMPACT of the result (1 - Very Low to 10 - Very High) EASE of achieving (1 - Very Difficult to 10 - Very Easy)

No.	Ideas/Actions/Countermeasures	EASE	IMPACT
1.			
2.			
3			
4.			
5.			
6.			
7.			

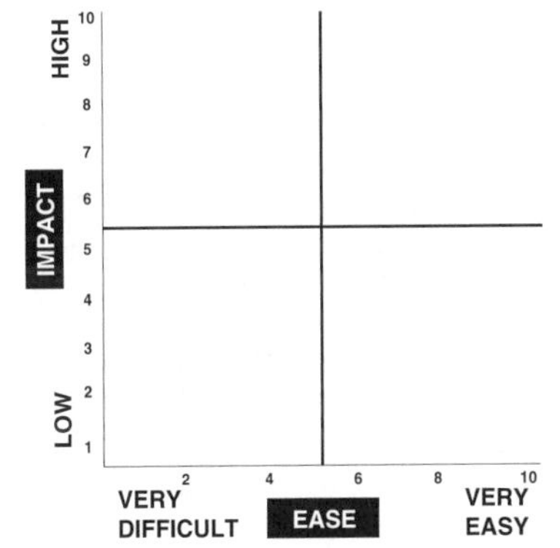

CHECK

Run Chart

A Run Chart, in its most simple form, is a method to display serial data points over time. Because our minds are not good at remembering patterns in data, a visual display will allow you to see the measurement(s) of an entire process. This in turn will enable you to see trends over time and to make adjustments accordingly. Interim Containment Actions and Permanent Countermeasures must be tracked to determine their overall effectiveness. For example, if an Interim Containment Action did not result in having an impact on the root cause, then that should not be part of any Permanent Countermeasure.

Run Charts will allow a team to compare performance measurements before and after implementation of a solution to measure its effectiveness. These charts focus attention on the vital changes determined by the previous tools used.

Approach creating a Run Chart as follows:

1. Label each Interim Containment Action and Permanent Countermeasure.
2. Create a graph denoting the vertical axis as 100 Percent of the problem being solved. If a target or benchmark has been the goal of the PDCA Kaizen Team, use that number. Create the horizontal axis with the dates from the Gantt Chart.
3. Use the data collected from the prototyping and trials and plot on the graph from the specific label from (1).
4. Continue to use the Impact Map and the brainstorming tool to analyze the results of the Run Chart.
5. Continue with the PDCA Kaizen Event methodology.

Case Study for the Run Chart - Meeting 3

The team decided to convey each Interim Containment Action (ICA) as well as Permanent Countermeasure (CM) with their corresponding reference number from the Countermeasure Kaizen Log (page 88). The team realized that the Interim Containment Actions did not have the immediate impact on improving the Customer Satisfaction Survey to 95% and all invoices being correct. This was due to additional problems within the fulfillment system and the difficulty the team had with implementing some of the Interim Containment Actions.

The following information is their Run Chart.

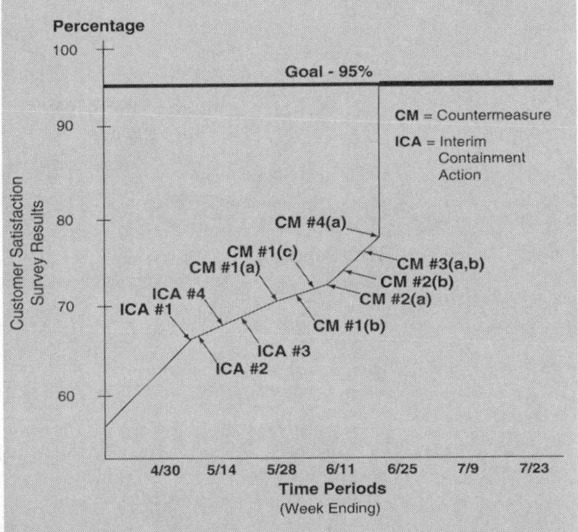

See pages 190-191 for a larger view of this worksheet.

CHECK

Use the following Run Chart worksheet with your team to monitor and track Interim Containment Actions, as well as Permanent Countermeasures.

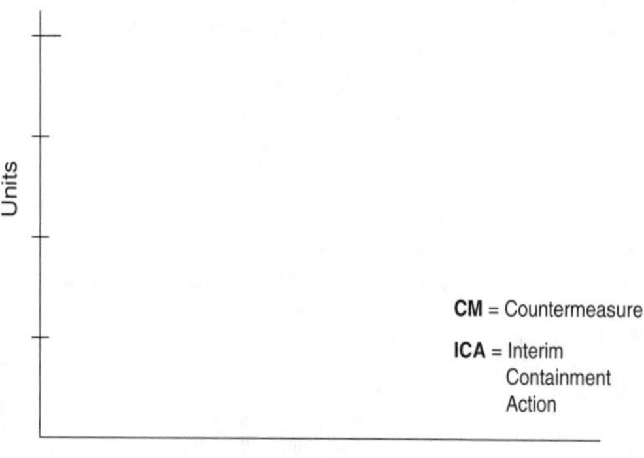

CHECK Readiness Guide

The questions listed below should be reviewed with the team to ensure all appropriate tools are completed (if appropriate) prior to implementing the next phase. A majority of the questions should be answered with a Yes.

Readiness Guide for CHECK

If you answer No to more than half of these, then consider using additional tools in the CHECK phase.

1. Are there correct measures in place to monitor the changes? ❒Yes ❒No
2. Have the actions (i.e., Interim, etc.) addressed the problem? ❒Yes ❒No
3. Has an Impact Map been created? ❒Yes ❒No
4. Has a Run Chart been created? ❒Yes ❒No
5. Has the Team Champion (or Sponsor) been updated? ❒Yes ❒No
6. Have visual controls been adequately used? ❒Yes ❒No
7. Have mistake proofing devices been adequately used? ❒Yes ❒No
8. Have new or changed standards been well documented? ❒Yes ❒No
9. Has a process been created to improve new or changed standards? ❒Yes ❒No
10. Are standard methods being implemented and documented? ❒Yes ❒No
11. Has everyone on the team contributed? ❒Yes ❒No
12. Has the A3 Report or Storyboard been updated? ❒Yes ❒No

Case Study for Lean Considerations

The team had success from each of the Interim Containment Actions as well as the Permanent Countermeasures. It was realized that there were numerous root causes to the problem of incorrect invoices. Most importantly, through the understanding of Lean with this team, and their subsequent use of some of the tools, improvements beyond their previous levels were attained. The challenge would be to ensure the improvements and solutions of the problems be sustained.

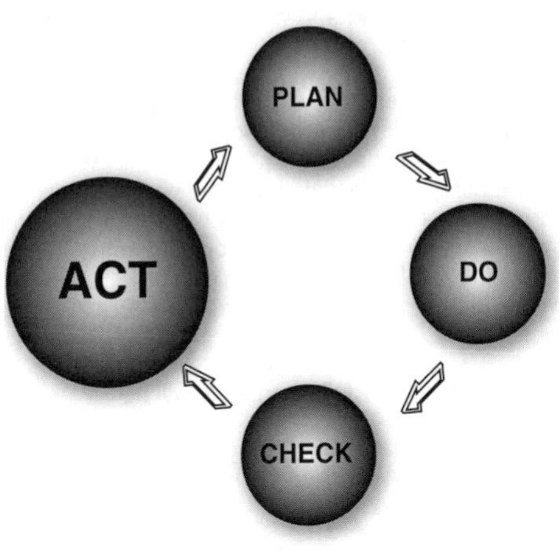
PLAN
DO
CHECK
ACT

ACT - *to adopt and update the necessary standards, abandon the process change, or run through the cycle again.*

The ACT stage of the PDCA process involves assessing the results from the PLAN, DO, and CHECK phases to determine what worked and what did not work. This may involve the following:

- Continuing with additional trials or beginning with the PLAN phase, if data is not conclusive
- Creating new standards
- Implementing pilot or trial enterprise wide (if applicable)
- Sharing the results through Yokotens and other intra-company avenues (newsletters, blogs, etc.)
- Completing the Storyboard to present in a Yokoten
- Celebrating the success among the PDCA Kaizen Team

In the ACT Phase, the following tools will be defined:

- ✔ Standard Work
- ✔ Performance Measurement
- ✔ Yokoten

The keys to the success of sustaining improvements is the ability of the PDCA Kaizen Team to:

1. Have work standards made visual
2. Create accurate process steps
3. Provide adequate training and simple measurements to ensure standards are followed

It is difficult to attain process consistency if workers are each doing tasks differently (i.e., with variation and the waste associated with it).

Standard Work

Standard work is a set of procedures that control tasks that are executed consistently - without variation from the original intent. Standard work provides a consistent basis for maintaining productivity, quality, and safety at a high level. (Kaizen will be the mechanism of continuing the improvement, as well as providing the human motivation of encouraging individuals to take part in designing and managing their own processes.)

Note: Most likely the PDCA Kaizen teams will be creating and/or modifying a current set of activities or tasks and not actually completing the two forms associated with the Lean tool of standard work (i.e., the Standard Work Combination Table and the Standard Work Chart). It is more important to establish a standard first and then use these tools for their improvement.

Approach standard work as follows:

1. Determine the best sequence of activities to meet customer demand (takt time). If takt time is not applicable, determine the time element in which the next process requires the service or information.
2. List the processes that require new or updated standards. This would include any Interim Containment Actions that would be Permanent Countermeasures.
3. Create an appropriate visual (i.e., flowcharts, digital photos, illustrations, etc.) that will support (2).
4. Create a training plan to ensure everyone is trained to the new process.
5. Measure productivity to ensure everyone is following the standard.
6. Create a system for improving the standard.
7. Continue with the PDCA Kaizen Event methodology.

Case Study for Standard Work - Meeting 3

The team realized that the customer service representatives, as well as many of the sales associates, had their own unique set of processes for handling certain customer orders. The team further decided to standardized this through creating standard work.

The following information is their Standard Work Guidelines Worksheet.

Standard Work Guidelines Worksheet

Note: If process cycle times need to be improved, consider using the Standard Work Combination Table.

No.	Process Name	ICA or CM #	Flowchart Available	Process Owner	Training Completed	Measurements in Place
1.	New Sales program	CM #1(b)	Yes	K.W.	Yes	Yes
2.	CSRs work loads - order entry	CM #2(c)	Yes	B.K.	Yes	Yes
3.	New fulfillment system process	CM #3(b)	Yes	J.I.	Yes	Yes
4.	On-line checklist	CM #4(a)	Yes	J.I.	Yes	Yes
5.						
6.						
7.						

See pages 194-195 for a larger view of this worksheet.

Use the following worksheet to document and consider visual controls in creating your standard work.

Standard Work Guidelines Worksheet

Note: If process cycle times need to be improved, consider using the Standard Work Combination Table.

No.	Process Name	ICA or CM #	Flowchart Available	Process Owner	Training Completed	Measurements in Place
1.						
2.						
3						
4.						
5.						
6.						
7.						

Performance Measurement

Performance measurements are the measurable indicators that can be systematically tracked to assess progress made in achieving predetermined goals and using such indicators to assess progress in achieving those goals. The purpose of measuring is not only to know how your business is performing but to allow it to perform better. The ultimate aim of implementing a performance measurement system is to improve performance

Modern organizations are complex systems, connecting a company's overarching objectives enabling managers and process workers to mobilize the appropriate resources and capabilities to ensure that it achieves its paramount goals. It shows managers both what they ought to measure and what they ought to do with the measures. For the PDCA Kaizen Event we are concerned only with the process level measurements, which should contribute to higher level measurement goals.

A good performance measurement system:

- Has improvement-oriented measures
- Provides no data without a rationale and purpose
- Ensures that employees (i.e., the process workers) know why things are being measured
- Ensures that employees know what to do about the measures if a negative trend occurs

There are many different types of measurements. Many times they will be part of a Balance Scorecard or Quality Dashboard. The Balance Scorecard and/or Quality Dashboard are a broad set of categories the organization is measured on. These measurements have goals and when a certain category is not meeting its goal, then resources (such as a PDCA Kaizen Event) are planned.

Performance Measurements are of three types.

1. Strategic Measures: market segmentation (industry structure, growth, ROI, concentration, innovation, customer loyalty, logistical complexity) and competitive strength (relative market share, quality, intellectual property, customer coverage), etc., to name a few
2. Organizational Measures: leanness, culture, incentives, training and development, etc., to name a few
3. Process Measures: customer satisfaction, product or service excellence, capacity utilization, capital intensity, productivity, cycle time, lead time, throughput, etc., to name a few

The PDCA Kaizen Event is concerned with the process measures to ensure the activities and countermeasures are successful. This data should be collected often and be visually displayed to show the progress of the various initiatives.

Approach Performance Measurements as follows:

1. Describe the need for performance measurements in relation to the Lean or Six Sigma project.
2. Describe the Interim Containment Actions and/or Permanent Countermeasures that are planned to address the problem.
3. Collect data daily (if appropriate) for each item listed in (2). (If one measurement will suffice for a group of activities, then note each activity.)
4. Create the appropriate visuals denoting the targets and anticipated results, if applicable.
5. Monitor data and make appropriate changes, if needed.
6. Continue with the PDCA Kaizen Event methodology.

Case Study for Performance Measurement - Meeting 3

The team decided to put in place measurements to review the Customer Satisfaction Survey as well as the number of incorrect invoices on a weekly basis.

The following information is their Performance Measurement Worksheet.

Performance Measurement Worksheet
1. Describe the need for this performance measurement. Incorrect invoices have a direct impact on the Customer Satisfaction Survey, as well as profitability and cash flow for the organization.
2. Describe the activities (containment actions, countermeasures) planned to address the need. 1. CM#1(c) will ensure proper discounts are credited to all invoices. 2. CM#3(b) will ensure orders are not shipped short, and if so, invoice will reflect actual shipment. 3. CM#4(a) will ensure orders and invoices over $5000 are correct.
3. How many people will participate in each activity? 1. CM#1(c) assigned to J.B. 2. CM#3(b) assigned to J.I. 3. CM#4(a) assigned to J.I.
4. When does the activity begin? 1. CM#1(c) 5/30 2. CM#3(b) 6/1 3. CM#4(a) 6/1
5. When does the activity end? 1. CM#1(c) 9/30 2. CM#3(b) 9/30 3. CM#4(a) 9/30
6. What are the targets and where are they posted. 1. CM#1(c) Reduction in invoicing errors by 33%; posted on Acct. bulletin board 2. CM#3(b) Reduction in invoicing errors by 33%; posted on Acct. bulletin board 3. CM#4(a) Reduction in invoicing errors by 33%; posted on Acct. bulletin board
7. Describe how the data will be collected. Frequency and by whom? 1. CM#1(c), manual review daily, C.M. 2. CM#3(b) 9/30, manual review daily, C.M. 3. CM#4(a) 9/30, manual review daily, C.M.
8. Combine your anticipated results and your targets in 1-2 sentences. Each of the three CMs most likley will reduce the 8% invoice errors to <2% within a three month period. The CMs will also increase the survey results to 90+%.

See pages 198-199 for a larger view of this worksheet.

Jse the following worksheet to document and consider isuals for creating your Performance Measurement Vorksheet.

Performance Measurement Worksheet
1. Describe the need for this performance measurement.
2. Describe the activities (containment actions, countermeasures) planned to address the need.
3. How many people will participate in each activity?
4. When does the activity begin?
5. When does the activity end?
6. What are the targets and where are they posted.
7. Describe how the data will be collected. Frequency and by whom?
8. Combine your anticipated results and your targets in 1-2 sentences.

Yokoten

Yokoten means "best practice sharing" or "taking from on place to another." It encompasses the methods of com municating, documenting, and distributing knowledg horizontally within an organization (peer-to-peer) abou what works and what doesn't work from an improvemer project (i.e., PDCA Kaizen Event). Yokoten is a form (knowledge management. At its most basic level, Yokote can be the notebook that a team keeps as a history of th group and problems/solutions encountered. Yokoten ca be the library of Storyboards (A3 Reports) that a team c work group maintains for all to access. As a knowledg management device, the Yokoten process ensures info mation becomes part of the *organizational* knowledg base. At Toyota there is an expectation that copying good idea will be followed by some added "kaizen" to tha idea (copy + kaizen = yokoten).

Yokoten standardizes a solution and shares it. Sharing c standard procedures across an organization is ideal.

Approach Yokotens as follows:

1. Create a standard improvement methodology tha problem solving, Lean, or Six Sigma teams will follov Ensure adequate training is conducted.
2. Create standard forms and worksheets to be usec Inform employees where these forms are located o the Local Area Network.
3. Assign a certain date and time each month (or quarte for groups and/or departments to share their PDC Kaizen Event failures and successes. Allocate 10-1 minutes per group (or representatives) to share the improvement projects.
4. Document all completed PDCA Kaizen Events on th network (LAN) or company intranet.
5. Ensure each team completes a Yokoten Workshee prior to their presentation.
6. Continue with additional PDCA Kaizen Events.

Case Study for Yokoten - Meeting 4

The team decided to share their success and struggles at an all-employee meeting that Kate had arranged. Kate wanted two team members to present the success of their Interim Containment Actions and Permanent Countermeasures. Jeff, from IT, and Juan, from HR, volunteered to present at the meeting.

The following is their Yokoten Worksheet.

Yokoten Worksheet

Problem: Incorrect invoices accounting for negative trend in Customer Satisfaction Survey results

Presentation Date: 9/1

List team members that will present at Yokoten meeting.
Jeff (IT), Juan (HR)

Convey pre- and post measurements in simple form.
Pre - 8% of all invoices incorrect
Post - <2% of all invoices are incorrect
Pre - 55% cust. sat. level
Post - 95% cust. sat. level

Place a check mark (✓) by each waste that was eliminated.

	Overproduction	✓	Overprocessing
	Waiting (Queues)		Inventory
✓	Motion	✓	Defects
	Transport		People's Skills

Convey timeline in simple bar graph form.

Permanent Countermeasures (#1a and #4a)		May	June
Update fulfillment system	20 days		
Create on-line checklist	10 days		

Place a check mark (✓) by the tools used. Identify the main tools used by placing a cirlce around each check mark.

	5S	✓	Effective Meetings	✓	Idea Kaizen	✓	Perf. Measurement		Takt Time
(✓)	5 Why Analysis		Effective Team	(✓)	Impact Map		Pitch	✓	Training Plan
	Accepting Change	(✓)	Failure Prev. Analysis		Just-In-Time	(✓)	Problem Identification		Value Stream Mapping
✓	Brainstorming	(✓)	Fishbone		Kanban		Pull Systems		Waste Audit
	Continuous Flow	✓	Flowchart		Mistake Proofing	(✓)	Run Chart		Work Load Balancing
	Cycle Time		Gantt Chart		Paper File System		Runners	(✓)	Yokoten
✓	Data Collection		Heijunka - Leveling	(✓)	Pareto	✓	Standard Work		

List any Idea Kaizens that were generated.
1. Create on-line check list for quotes
2. All orders follow same process, no exceptions
3.

List recommendations to management.
1. More training on Lean tools
2. More of same type of events to improve processes
3.

List a few experiences regarding the four stages of team development.
1. Orginally thought it was all IT's problem
2. Sales very helpful in creating new on-line system
3.

List recommendations to other teams.
1. Ensure problem is clearly identified
2. Each team member to receive at least one action item
3.

List overall benefits from the PDCA Kaizen Event.
1. Achieved goal
2. Process permanently improved
3. All team members felt they contributed

List contact person and email for additional information.
Jeff Ito, IT, 745-665-1212, jeff.ito@tinkertowninc.com

List where the electronic version of the Yokoten, as well as the supporting materials, are located for future reference.
All forms, worksheets for this project are located: H:Yokoten/May_CustomerSurveyImprovements

See pages 202-203 for a larger view of this worksheet.

ACT

Use the following worksheet or something similar as a guide to adequately present your Lean or Six Sigma project to the organization.

Yokoten Worksheet

Problem: ____________ **Presentation Date:** ____________

List team members that will present at Yokoten meeting.

Convey pre- and post measurements in simple form.

Place a check mark (✓) by each waste that was eliminated.

	Overproduction		Overprocessing
	Waiting (Queues)		Inventory
	Motion		Defects
	Transport		People's Skills

Convey timeline in simple bar graph form.

Place a check mark (✓) by the tools used. Identify the main tools used by placing a circle around each check mark.

	5S		Effective Meetings		Idea Kaizen		Perf. Measurement		Takt Time
	5 Why Analysis		Effective Team		Impact Map		Pitch		Training Plan
	Accepting Change		Failure Prev. Analysis		Just-In-Time		Problem Identification		Value Stream Mapping
	Brainstorming		Fishbone		Kanban		Pull Systems		Waste Audit
	Continuous Flow		Flowchart		Mistake Proofing		Run Chart		Work Load Balancing
	Cycle Time		Gantt Chart		Paper File System		Runners		Yokoten
	Data Collection		Heijunka - Leveling		Pareto		Standard Work		

List any Idea Kaizens that were generated. 1. 2. 3.	List recommendations to management. 1. 2. 3.
List a few experiences regarding the four stages of team development. 1. 2. 3.	List recommendations to other teams. 1. 2. 3.
List overall benefits from the PDCA Kaizen Event. 1. 2. 3.	List contact person and email for additional information.
List where the electronic version of the Yokoten, as well as the supporting materials, are located for future reference.	

ACT

Case Study - In Conclusion - Meeting 5

Kate had repeatedly mentioned throughout the meetings that this was not going to be the only Kaizen Event - and that the company needed to focus on continuous improvement - not just when a problem arises.

The results from the 3 month improvement project were that customer satisfaction survey level increased to 95% - a level never seen by Tinker Town, Inc. Also, invoicing errors were reduced by nearly 400%, from 8% to less than 2%.

Kate summarized the Kaizen Event to the team by saying, "This was a new beginning for Tinker Town and everyone contributed to its success. We will continue to problem solve and learn more about Lean as we go forward. We will build upon what we learned and include more employees in additional Kaizen Events to create new customer service survey levels, as well as reduce invoicing errors even further. But, just to let you know, we did implement some some Lean tools in this Kaizen Event. The tools of standard work, visual controls, mistake proofing, and Just-In-Time information were used in this project. You are all to be commended on your participation. I look forward your participation in upcoming improvement projects."

Kate awarded each team member with a $50.00 gift certificate from Olive Garden, along with a handshake and a personal thank you.

Note: Kate realized that they had improved one value stream - the customer invoicing process, but realized many other value streams needed to be improved (e.g., the quote-to-order, custom product order, standard teddy bear manufacturing, etc.). However, Tinker Town, Inc. had a successful first step in their never-ending journey of continuous improvement.

See page 210 for additional explanation of the Lean tools mentioned previously in the case study.

ACT Readiness Guide

The questions listed below should be reviewed with the team to ensure all appropriate tools are completed (if appropriate) prior to implementing the next phase. A majority of the questions should be answered with a Yes.

Readiness Guide for ACT

If you answer No to more than half of these, then consider using additional tools in the ACT phase.

1. Have the changes proven successful given the identified problem? ❒Yes ❒No
2. Is the importance to standard work understood by everyone? ❒Yes ❒No
3. Have proven actions been documented to best practice? ❒Yes ❒No
4. Have Performance Measures been identified for system wide roll-out? ❒Yes ❒No
5. Has the Team Champion (or Sponsor) been updated? ❒Yes ❒No
6. Has the Standard Work Guidelines Worksheet been reviewd by all? ❒Yes ❒No
7. Has a timeline been created for system wide implementation? ❒Yes ❒No
8. Is the Training Plan being followed? ❒Yes ❒No
9. Are there plans for a 30-60-90 day review? ❒Yes ❒No
10. If actions did not solve the problem, is the team ready to start over? ❒Yes ❒No
11. If the team must start at the PLAN phase, does everyone know why? ❒Yes ❒No
12. Has a Yokoten been planned? ❒Yes ❒No
12. Has the A3 Report or Storyboard been updated? ❒Yes ❒No

Storyboard (A3 Report)

PDCA Kaizen Project Name: Customer Survey Imp

Team Members: Kate, Juan, Jeff, Judy, Susan, Bob, an

Problem Identification

WHO: External customers (Survey Results)
WHAT: Billing errors
WHERE: Invoices
WHY: Invoices incorrect
HOW: Sales input, discounts
QUANTITY: 8% of all invoices

Data Chart of Present Condition
(from Data Check Sheet and/or Pareto)

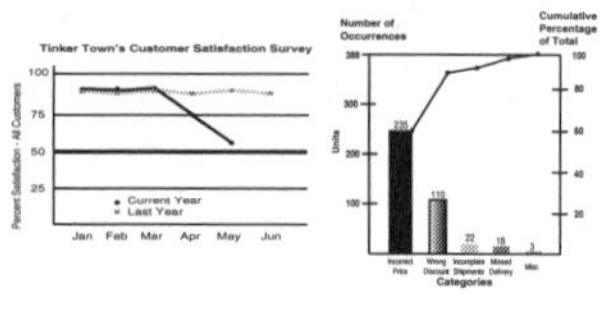

Goal / Standard

100% Correct Invoices
98% Customer Satisfaction Survey

Waste(s) Indentified

- [ ] Overproduction
- [x] Waiting
- [x] Motion
- [ ] Transport
- [ ] Overprocessing
- [ ] Inventory (Time)
- [x] Defects (Correction of)
- [x] People's Skills

Measurement(s) Affected

Customer Satisfaction, Profitability, Cash Flow

Fi

"Bone

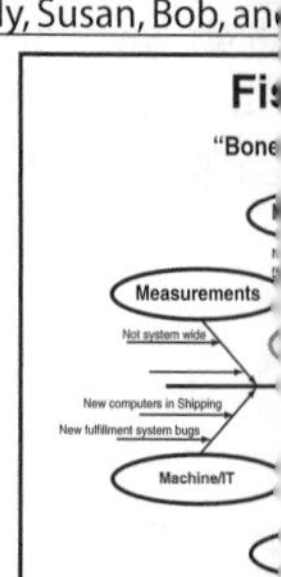

Coun
(Actions f

Interim Co
Acti

MAN

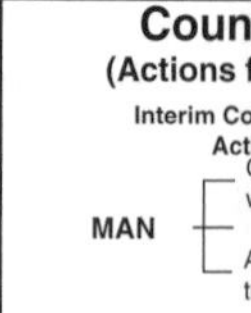

MATERIAL

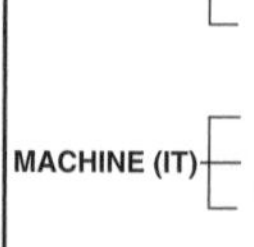

MACHINE (IT)

METHOD

Storyboard (A3 Report)

Date: August 31st

Value Stream: Customer Order to Invoicing

iagram

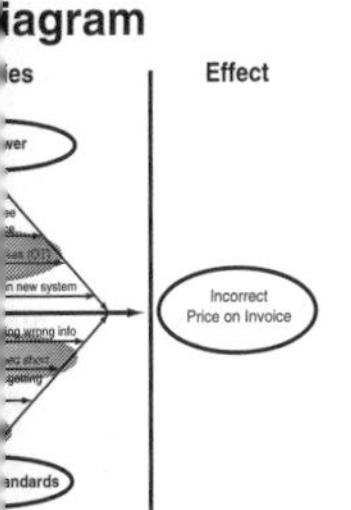

Results

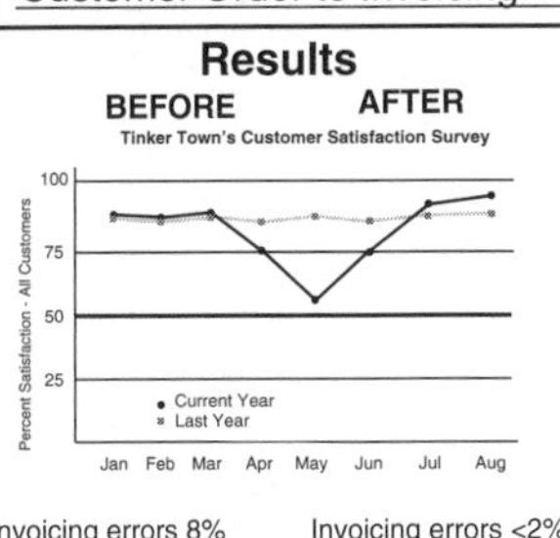

Invoicing errors 8% — Invoicing errors <2%

measures
5 Why analysis)

Permanent Countermeasure Actions

- Create training plan for CSRs
- Create standard work

- Create new Sales update program
- Mistake Proof IT prod. discounts
- Create on-line checlist

- Update new fulfillment system
- Determine takt time

Standardization

Process owners identfied and standard work procedures created.

Standard Work Charts used in training and posted at each CSR's desk.

Yokoten Review Date

September 1 - 1:00pm - 2:30pm

Recognition

Team lunch on August 12th at Olive Garden and

$50.00 Gift Cards from Olive Garden.

Next Target

Achieve 98% customer satisfaction and reduce invoicing errors to <1%.

Waste Audit

Waste Category	Definition	Examples
Overproduction	This waste is producing work or providing a service prior to it being required or requested. This is the greatest of all the wastes. In that, if you overproduce some type of work or service, it encompasses many of the other wastes.	Producing work units ahead of schedule Duplicate files Producing reports no one reads or needs Making extra copies Printing, e-mailing, sending, or faxing the same document twice
Waiting (Time in Queue)	Waiting for anything – people, signatures, information, etc. - is waste. This waste of waiting is considered the "low hanging fruit". It is easy to identify and ripe for the taking. We often don't think of paper sitting in an In-basket as waste. However, when looking for an item, how many times do we mull through the In-basket to try and find it? How many times do you actually touch something before it is completed? It's the finish it, file it, or throw it away system that can help with eliminating this waste.	Parts or information not available Excessive signatures or approvals Dependency on others to complete tasks Delays in receiving information Computer program version problems Cross-departmental resource commitments
Motion	Any movement of people, paper, electronic exchanges (e-mails, etc.) that does not add value is waste. This waste can be created by poor office layout or design, ineffective office equipment, supplies located afar, etc.	Searching for parts, information, etc. Searching for computer files on your desktop Searching for work documents (files) Reviewing manuals for informatior Hand-carrying paperwork to another department or process
Transport	Transport is an important and ubiquitous element. It affects the delivery of any work within the office. It is the movement of work that does not add value.	Delivering parts or work document that are not required Excessive filing of work document E-mail distribution lists that are not up-to-date

To Detect This Waste Ask	Notes for Your Target Area
Is this work being performed ahead of schedule? Is this form a duplicate of some other form? Can the information on this form be used in other areas? Is someone using all the information that is being provided?	
Are there delays in the delivery of work or information? Are there issues with punctuality with internal, as well as external, customers? Are there certain times when delays are more prevalent? Is there a bottleneck in the process? Have delays always been a problem or are they a recent development?	
Can walking be reduced by repositioning equipment and/or supplies? Is the information required to do the work easily accessible? Are new and current employees properly trained in the process? Are prodedures in place for all critical processes? Are there certain areas that impede work flow?	
Is the information or work that is being transformed being hand-delivered to other processes? Is work being delivered to the right place at the right time? Has work been consolidated where appropriate?	

Waste Category	Definition	Examples
Overprocessing	Putting more work or effort into the work required by internal or external customers is waste. Excessive processing does not add value for the customer and the customer will not pay for it. This is one of the most difficult wastes to uncover.	Duplicate reports or information Repetitive data entry Incorrect information being shared Unnecessary enhancements to work units Duplicate documentation Lack of accurate project planning
Inventory	Work piles, excessive supplies, and excessive signature requirements are waste. They all take up space or require someone's time. This type of waste is fairly easy to spot.	Files/charts awaiting signatures or approvals Work awaiting task completion by other(s) Obsolete files Obsolete equipment Insufficient training of back-ups Purchasing excessive supplies Overstocking
Defects (Correction of)	Defect waste refers to all processing required in creating a defect and the additional work required to correct a defect. Defects (either internal or external) result in additional processing that will add no value to the product or service. It takes less time to do work correctly the first time than it would take to do it over. Rework is waste and adds more cost to any product or service. This waste can also reduce profits significantly.	Data entry errors Wrong billing code Pricing errors Forwarding incomplete documentation Lost files or records Not following up-to-date prints Incorrect information on documents Insufficient staffing to service customer
People's Skills	Many times this is the 8th waste. The underutilization of people is a result of not placing people where they can (and will) use their knowledge, skills, and abilities to the fullest. Use company policies and procedures to effectively place people where they will most benefit the organization.	Project deadlines not being met Work loads not evenly balanced due to lack of cross-training High absenteeism and turnover Incomplete job skill assessment prior to hiring Little contributions to improvement initiatives

To Detect This Waste Ask	Notes for Your Target Area
Has this work been done before? Is this a repeat of some earlier work? Has someone confirmed that this is exactly what the customer requested? Is there more information obtained than what is required? Are there redundant phone calls or e-mails when obtaining information?	
Are there boxes of material sitting on the floor? Are you using the hall for storage? Are there out-dated manuals in the area? Are internal or external customers waiting for information/work or a service to be provided? Is everyone working to their full capacity?	
Are there well-documented standard processes? Does equipment have a maintenance schedule? Are there effective cross-training programs? Do employees have the proper amount of time to do their work?	
Are employees effectively cross-trained? Are employees encouraged to suggest improvements? Are employees empowered to implement improvements? Are new employees trained to best practice?	

Forms and Worksheets

The following pages contain the forms and worksheets used throughout *Simply Lean* in a larger format for you to photocopy and enlarge. They are also available in the Kaizen Event Forms and Worksheets Microsoft Excel package at
www.theleanstore.com.

Idea Kaizen Form

Name:____________________ Department:______________

Upstream Customer:______________ Downstream Customer:______________

Step 1: Describe the Problem. Date:__________

Include photos, charts, and graphs, if necessary.

Step 2: Describe the Action to be Taken. Date: ____________

Include photos, charts, and graphs, if necessary.

Step 3: Follow-up. Did the Action Work? ❒ Yes ❒ No Date: ____________

Include photos, charts, and graphs, if necessary.
Additional Notes:

Effective Meeting Evaluation Worksheet

Directions:

1. Spend only five minutes evaluating your meetings.
2. This form is most successful when everyone's responses are shared.
3. Focus on the weak spots, applaud the high ratings.

Rating System: 1 is the lowest score (Poor) and 5 is the highest (Excellent) **Poor** **1 2 3 4 5** **Excellent**	**Score**
1. How well did we stay on the agenda?	
2. Are we focusing on the right issues during the meeting?	
3. How well did we look for problems in the process, rather than the person?	

4. How well did we use our time?	
5. How well did we discuss information? How clearly? How accurately?	
6. How well did we all participate?	
7. Was the meeting effective?	
8. How was the pace, flow, and tone of the meeting? (Did we get bogged down or stuck?)	
9. How well did we respond to each other's questions and comments?	
10. In general, were all ideas explored to the extent possible given the time element?	
TOTAL:	
Please provide any other comments or suggestions for improvements.	

Problem Identification Worksheet

Symptom: ____________________ Date Opened: ____________________

Problem Description: ____________________

____

Waste Created: ____________________ Measurements Affected: ____________________

Is/Is Not Questions	IS	IS NOT
What Object		
Where Seen on object		

When First seen When else seen		
How Large How many objects have defects		
Trend Increasing or decreasing over time		

Problem Identification Worksheet

Symptom: Customer complaints

Date Opened: 6/1

Problem Description: The Customer Survey has gone from 90% (March) to 75% in April and 55% in May.

Waste Created: Defects, Motion

Measurements Affected: Cash Generation, Profitability, Customer Sat. Survey

Is/Is Not Questions	IS	IS NOT
What **Object**	Customer Sat. Survey	Audits, quotes, etc.
Where **Seen on object**	On customer surveys	Quotes, expense reports, pick lists, etc.
When **First seen**	4/2	Prior to 4/2

When else seen	4/2 - 5/18	Prior to 4/2
How Large **How many objects have defects**	55% of surveys	45% of surveys
Trend **Increasing or decreasing over time**	Increasing	Decreasing

Data Check Sheet

Data Collection: ______ to ______ Process Area: ________________
(Mo/Day/Yr) (Mo/Day/Yr)

Location: ________________

Name(s): ________________

Reason/Attribute	Dates							Totals

Totals								

Data Check Sheet

Data Collection: 4/2 (Mo/Day/Yr) to 5/18 (Mo/Day/Yr) Area/Dept./Co.: Tinker Town, Inc.

Location: Santa Claus, Ind.

Name(s): Jeff and Linda

Reason/Attribute	Dates/Week Ending							Totals
	4/6	4/13	4/20	4/27	5/4	5/11	5/18	
Incorrect Price	35	28	36	23	40	31	42	235
Wrong Discount	13	18	15	19	14	19	12	110
Incomplete Shipment	0	0	7	10	0	5	0	22
Missed Delivery Date	0	0	0	18	0	0	0	18
Miscellaneous	0	0	0	0	3	0	0	3

Totals	48	46	58	70	57	55	54	388

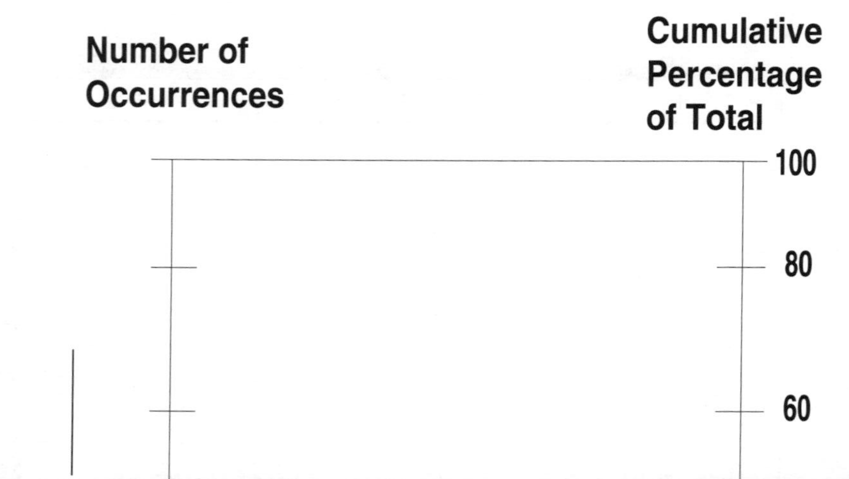
Number of Occurrences
Cumulative Percentage of Total
100
80
60

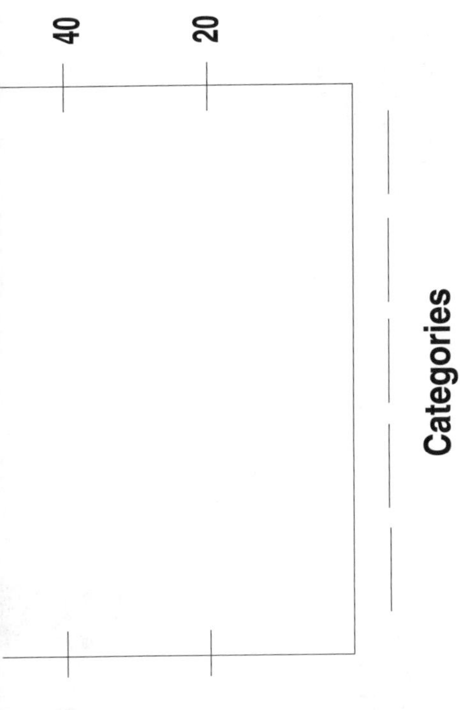
40
20
Categories
Units

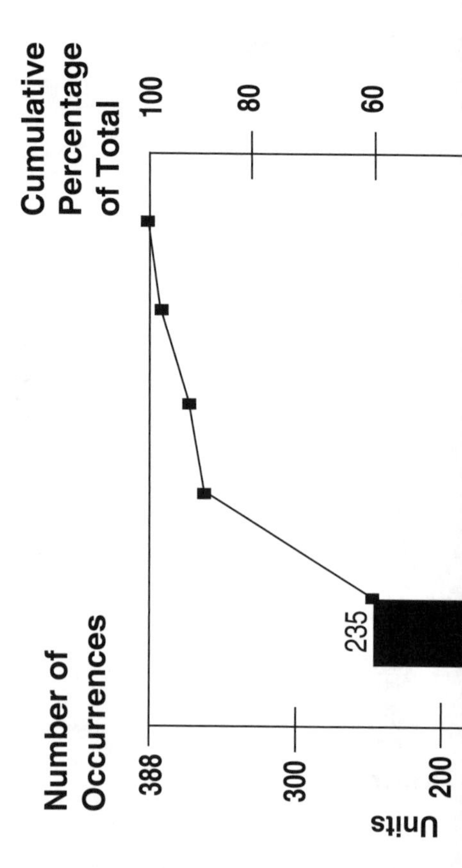

Cumulative Percentage of Total
100
80
60
Number of Occurrences
Units
388
300
200
235

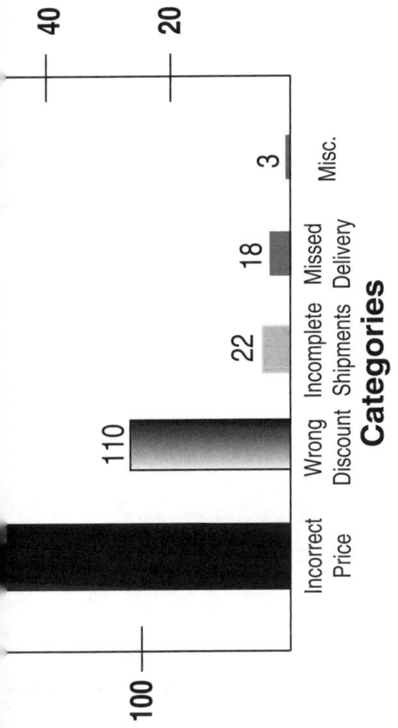

40
20
100
Incorrect Price
Wrong Discount
Incomplete Shipments
Missed Delivery
Misc.
110
22
18
3
Categories

Brainstorming Worksheet

Date: ________ Facilitator: ____________________

Topic: ____

List below the potential reasons.

✔
✔
✔
✔
✔
✔
✔
✔
✔
✔
✔
✔

Brainstorming Worksheet

Date: 5/18 Facilitator: Juan

Topic: Why customers have complained that their invoices are not correct.

List below the potential reasons.

- ✔ New fulfillment system not working correctly
- ✔ New bar code readers
- ✔ New sales manager
- ✔ New computers in Shipping
- ✔ Customer Service Representatives not trained
- ✔ New product line of Teddy Bears
- ✔ Customers not using current system correctly
- ✔ Discount schedules not updated regularly
- ✔ Quantity discounts for new products not immediately known
- ✔ Current customer discounts always changing
- ✔ New shipping vendor not connected to system

- ✔ Four retirements
- ✔ Customer Service Representatives entering wrong info
- ✔ Customer Service Representatives overworked
- ✔ Customer Service Representatives not receiving some orders until end of day
- ✔ No avenue for customer order quotes when sales info is not available
- ✔ Customers entering wrong information and Tinker Town accepts as order
- ✔ Supervisors not checking orders
- ✔ Orders over $5000 not following signature process
- ✔ Customers entering wrong discount and new system not verifying it
- ✔ Orders mixed up and customers receiving wrong orders
- ✔ Pick list for customers not accurate
- ✔ New merchant account not transferring order information correctly
- ✔ Part time employee in customer service not trained adequately

"Bones" Major Cause

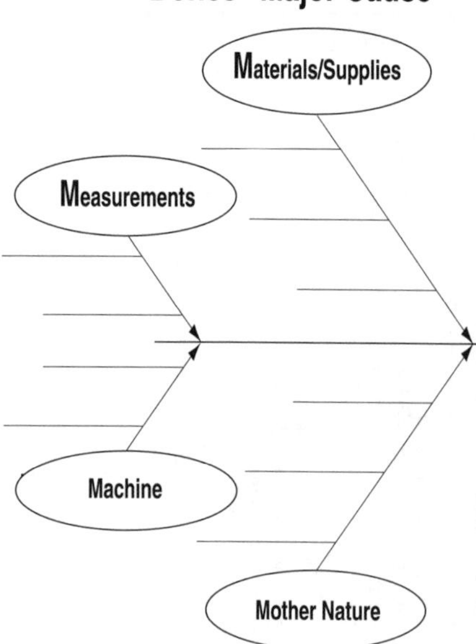

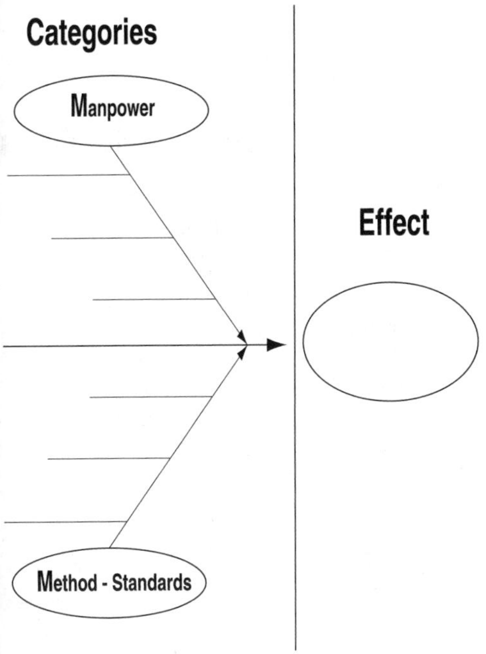
Categories
Manpower
Effect
Method - Standards

"Bones" Major Caus

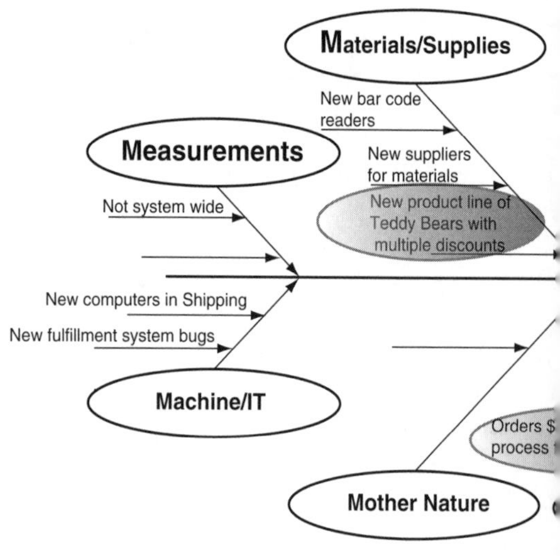

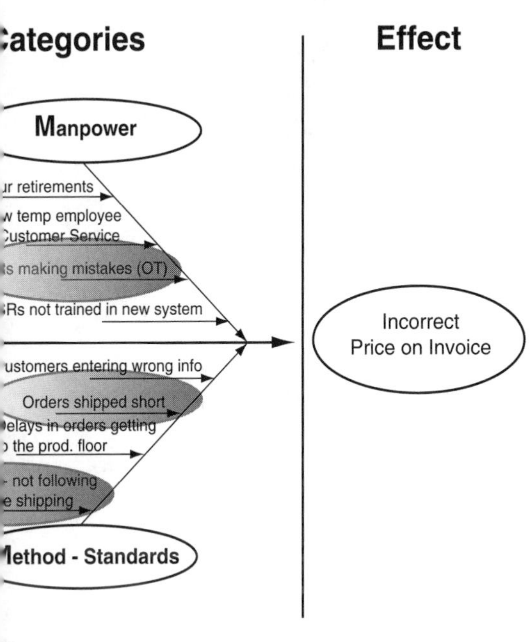

:ategories
Effect
Manpower
ır retirements
w temp employee
:ustomer Service
ts making mistakes (OT)
;Rs not trained in new system
ustomers entering wrong info
Orders shipped short
Delays in orders getting
› the prod. floor
- not following
e shipping
/lethod - Standards
Incorrect
Price on Invoice

5 Why Analysis

Problem: ____________

Cause	Cause	Cause	Cause
Why?	Why?	Why?	Why?
Why?	Why?	Why?	Why?

Why?	Why?	Why?	Why?
Why?	Why?	Why?	Why?
Why?	Why?	Why?	Why?

5 Why Analysis

Problem: Incorrect Prices on Invoices

Cause	Cause	Cause	Cause
CSRs making mistakes (OT)	Orders shipped short	Orders over $5000 not following process	New product line with multiple discounts
Why? Always had large group of orders at the end of the day	**Why?** Not enough inventory to meet demand	**Why?** Orders were not separated	**Why?** Software not configured properly
Why? Intl orders processed at 1:00pm daily and CSRs could not adapt to large orders	**Why?** Production did not have up-to-date inventory levels	**Why?** Sales informed shipping to ship regardless of credit	**Why?** Did not include account special information as well as new customer fields

Why? New system was not updated and only CSRs were trained in new system	**Why?** New fulfillment system only updates bi-weekly	**Why?** Sales knew that new system would cause delays	**Why?** No one was assigned to ensure information would work in new fulfillment system
Why? IT was not aware of Intl orders being processed only at 1:00pm daily	**Why?** Standard feature on new fulfillment system	**Why?** Sales wanted to ensure customer demand be met	**Why?** Four retirements caused workers to absorb as much work as possible
Why? IT did not realize this batching of orders and being short in CS caused addl OT	**Why?**	**Why?**	**Why?**

Flowchart Worksheet

Use the following standard symbols to represent the process flow.

Symbol	Meaning	Symbol	Meaning	Symbol	Meaning
⬭	Start or end of process	▭	Document	→	Direction of process flow
▭	Task or activity	▭	Multiple documents	D	Delay, queue time
◇	Decisions - branches	▭	Standard or protocol	○	Connector

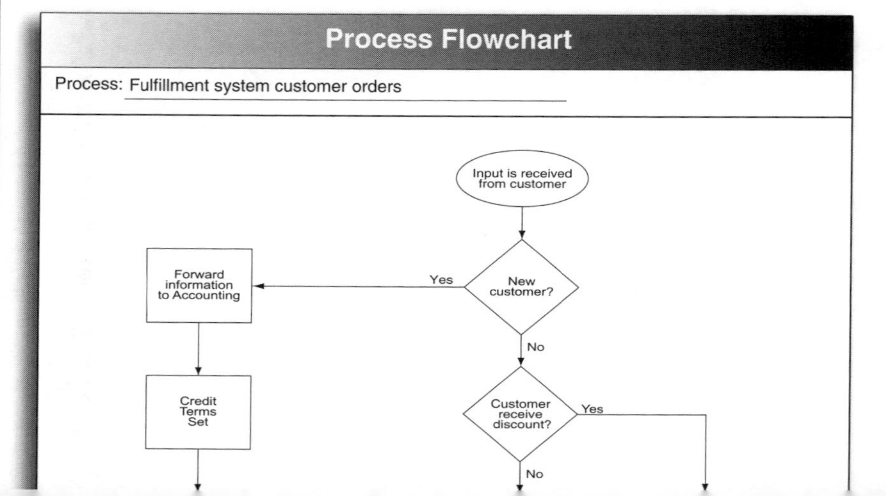
Process Flowchart
Process: Fulfillment system customer orders
Input is received from customer
New customer?
Yes
No
Forward information to Accounting
Credit Terms Set
Customer receive discount?
Yes
No

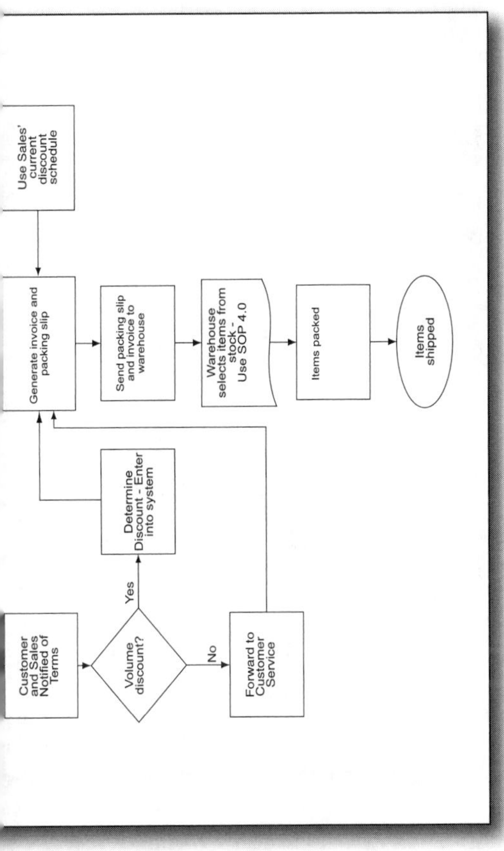
Customer and Sales Notified of Terms
Volume discount?
Yes
No
Determine Discount - Enter into system
Forward to Customer Service
Use Sales' current discount schedule
Generate invoice and packing slip
Send packing slip and invoice to warehouse
Warehouse selects items from stock - Use SOP 4.0
Items packed
Items shipped

Managing Change Checklist

Directions:

1. Spend only a few minutes reviewing this checklist.
2. Use the checklist with the PDCA Kaizen team prior to rolling out any changes.
3. Focus on the weak spots that have scores less than 3.

Rating System: 1 is the lowest score (Poor) and 5 is the highest (Excellent) **Poor 1 2 3 4 Excellent 5**	**Score**
1. Is there a clear and compelling reason for adopting this improvement?	
2. Is objective data available to convince any skeptics?	
3. Do people feel the urgency for this change?	
4. Are the motivators known for each person affected by the change?	
5. Does the senior executive team support this change?	

6. Has the proposed change been communicated to all stakeholders?	
7. Are the right people selected for the right roles?	
8. Are performance measurements and reporting systems made visual for the change?	
9. Is the training plan adequately resourced?	
10. Are project management principles and methods being used (i.e., Team Charter, Agendas, Timelines, etc.)?	
11. Is support in place, ensuring transfer of training to the workplace (i.e., standards of work)?	
12. Are successes celebrated?	
13. Have I (we) studied the changes carefully and identified if anyone is likely to lose something -- including what I (we) may be likely to lose?	
14. What actions can I (we) take to help people deal more successfully with the changes that are taking place with this PDCA Kaizen Event? What can I (we) do today to get started on this aspect of the change?	
TOTAL:	

Countermeasures Kaizen Log

Problem: ______________________ Date: ____________

Causes	Interim Containment Actions	WHO	START DATE	TARGET	END DATE
1.	1.				
	1.				
2.	2.				
	2.				
3.	3.				
	3.				
4.	4.				
	4.				

	Permanent Countermeasures	WHO	START DATE	TARGET	END DATE
1.	1. 1.				
2.	2. 2.				
3.	3. 3.				
4.	4. 4.				

Countermeasures Kaizen Log

Problem: Customer Survey negative trend due to 8% of all invoices incorrect **Date:** 5/22

Causes	Interim Containment Actions	WHO	START DATE	END DATE
1. New product line w/ mult. discounts	a. Create manual system w/ Sales	B.K.	5/22	6/28
2. CSRs making mistakes (OT)	b. Assign data input to those trained	W.B.	5/22	6/15
3. Orders shipped short	c. Supervisors to check all orders and invoices	D.T.	5/22	6/24
4. Orders over $5000+ not following process	d. Create red folder for orders over $5000 and include checklist before shipping	J.B.	5/22	6/24

	Permanent Countermeasures	WHO	START DATE	END DATE
1. New product line w/ mult. discounts	a. Update new fulfillment system	J.I.	6/1	6/30
	b. Create new Sales update program	K.W.	5/22	6/22
	c. Create Mistake Proofing IT solution for product discounts	J.B.	5/30	6/15
2. CSRs making mistakes (OT)	a. Create training plan for all CSRs and implement	W.B.	6/1	6/8
	b. Determine takt time and pitch for customer orders	B.K.	5/30	6/4
	c. Create standard work and balance work loads	B.K.	5/30	6/15
3. Orders shipped short	a. Create Standard Work Chart and post	R.H.	6/15	6/30
	b. Update fulfillment system to verify order and price disc.	J.I.	6/1	6/15
4. Orders over $5000+ not following process	a. Create a visual control on-line checklist and train everyone	J.I.	6/1	6/15
	b. Value stream map the process for further analysis	K.W.	6/15	6/30

Failure Prevention Analysis Worksheet

Directions:

1. List all potential failures.
2. Assign a number from 1 to 10 for the potential and consequence of an activity going wrong.
3. Multiply the potential and consequence and rank from highest to lowest.

No chance for error or no consequence								High chance of error and great consequence	
1	2	3	4	5	6	7	8	9	10

Potential Failure	Potential	Consequence	Overall Rating	Ranking
A.				
B.				
C.				
D.				

E.				
F.				
G.				
H.				
I.				

Please provide any other comments or suggestions for improvements.

Failure Prevention Analysis Worksheet

Directions:

1. List all potential failures.
2. Assign a number from 1 to 10 for the potential and consequence of an activity going wrong.
3. Multiply the potential and consequence and rank from highest to lowest.

No chance for error or no consequence									High chance of error and great consequence
1	2	3	4	5	6	7	8	9	10

Potential Failure	Potential	Consequence	Overall Rating	Ranking
A. Create manual system w/ Sales	**4**	**8**	**32**	**4**
B. Assign data input to only those trained	**3**	**7**	**21**	**2**
C. Supervisors to check all orders and invoices	**7**	**9**	**63**	**6**

D. Create red folder for orders over $5000 and include checklist	6	9	54	5
E. Update new fulfillment system	2	9	18	1
F. Create new Sales update program	3	9	27	3
G.				
H.				
I.				

Please provide any other comments or suggestions for improvements.

The team decided to have the supervisors assign a back-up person to assist them in checking all orders. It was acknowledged that due to the retirements they have been exceptionally busy.

Training Plan Worksheet

Problem: ______________________ **Date:** ____________

Causes	INTERIM CONTAINMENT ACTIONS/ PERMANENT COUNTERMEASURES	TRAINEE(S)	TRAINER	MATERIALS REQUIRED	START DATE	LOCATION

Training Plan Worksheet

Problem: Customer Survey negative trend due to 8% of all invoices incorrect **Date:** 5/30

Causes	INTERIM CONTAINMENT ACTIONS/ PERMANENT COUNTERMEASURES	TRAINEE(S)	TRAINER	MATERIALS REQUIRED	START DATE	LOCATION
1. New product line w/ mult. discounts	1. Create manual system w/ Sales	Mkt, Sales,CS	B.K.	Excel	5/24	Sales Conf. Rm
3. Orders shipped short	3. Supervisors to check all orders and invoices	Sups.	D.T.	Visual Aid	5/26	Sales Conf. Rm
4. Orders over $5000+ not following process	4. Create red folder for orders over $5000 and include checklist	Sups./ Shipping	J.B.	Folders/ Labels	5/26	Training Room

1. New product line w/ mult. discounts	1. Update new fulfillment system 1. Create new Sales update program 1. Create Mistake Proofing IT solution	Mkt, Sales,CS	K.W.	Screen Printouts	6/15	Sales Conf. Rm
3. Orders shipped short	3. Create Standard Work Chart and post 3. Update fulfillment system.	CS/ Shipping	J.I.	Stand. Wrk.Chart	6/15	Training Room

Gantt Chart Worksheet

No.	Task Name	Duration	Time Interval (Days/Weeks/Months)			
1.						
2.						
3.						

4.
5.
6.
7.
8.

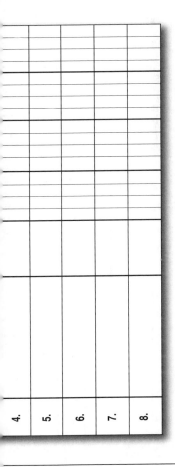

Gantt Chart Worksheet						
No.	Task Name	Duration	May	June	July	August
1.	Create Manual System	25 days				
2.	Assign data input	20 days				
3.	Sups. check orders/invoices	20 days				
4.	Create red folders	20 days				

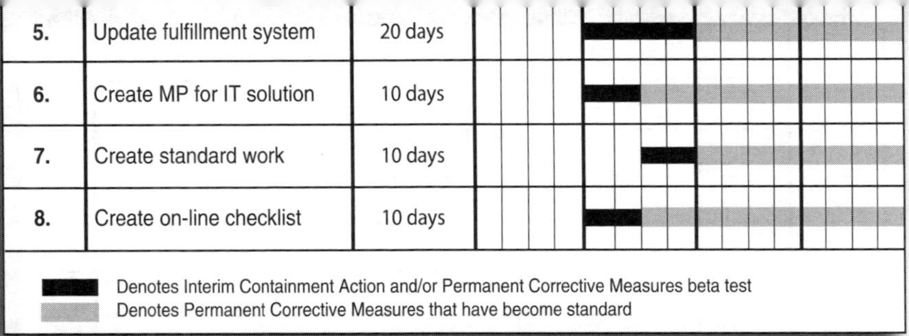

5.	Update fulfillment system	20 days
6.	Create MP for IT solution	10 days
7.	Create standard work	10 days
8.	Create on-line checklist	10 days

Denotes Interim Containment Action and/or Permanent Corrective Measures beta test
Denotes Permanent Corrective Measures that have become standard

Impact Map Worksheet

IMPACT of the result (1 - Very Low to 10 - Very High) EASE of achieving (1 - Very Difficult to 10 - Very Easy)

No.	Ideas/Actions/Countermeasures	EASE	IMPACT
1.			
2.			
3			
4.			
5.			
6.			
7.			

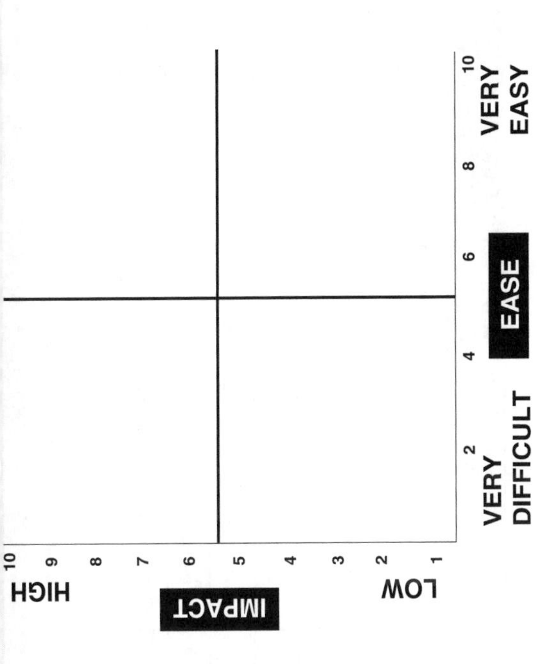

IMPACT
HIGH
LOW
10
9
8
7
6
5
4
3
2
1
EASE
VERY DIFFICULT
VERY EASY
2
4
6
8
10

Impact Map Worksheet

IMPACT of the result (1 - Very Low to 10 - Very High) EASE of achieving (1 - Very Difficult to 10 - Very Easy)

No.	Ideas/Actions/Countermeasures	EASE	IMPACT
1.	Update new fulfillment system	2	9
2.	Create new Sales update program	3	6
3	Create IT solutions for discounts	2	10
4.	Create training plan for CSRs	10	3
5.	Create standard work and balance work loads	8	8
6.	Update fulfillment system to verify order and price discounts	7	9
7.	Create visual control for on-line checklist and train everyone	9	7

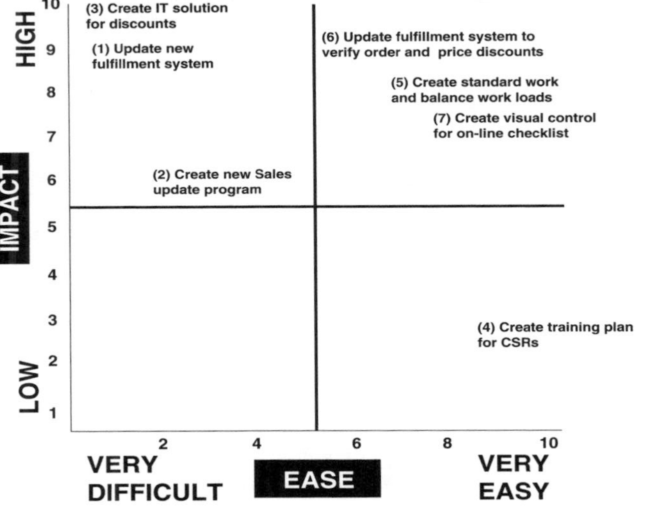

HIGH
IMPACT
LOW
10
9
8
7
6
5
4
3
2
1
(3) Create IT solution for discounts
(1) Update new fulfillment system
(2) Create new Sales update program
(6) Update fulfillment system to verify order and price discounts
(5) Create standard work and balance work loads
(7) Create visual control for on-line checklist
(4) Create training plan for CSRs
2
4
6
8
10
VERY DIFFICULT
EASE
VERY EASY

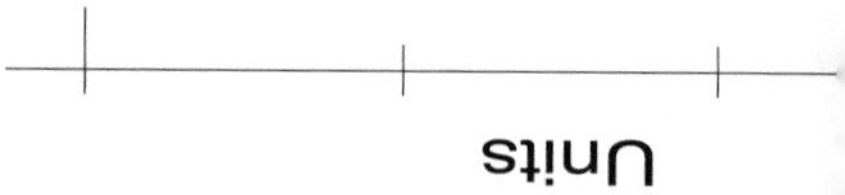

Units

CM = Countermeasure

ICA = Interim Containment Action

Time Periods

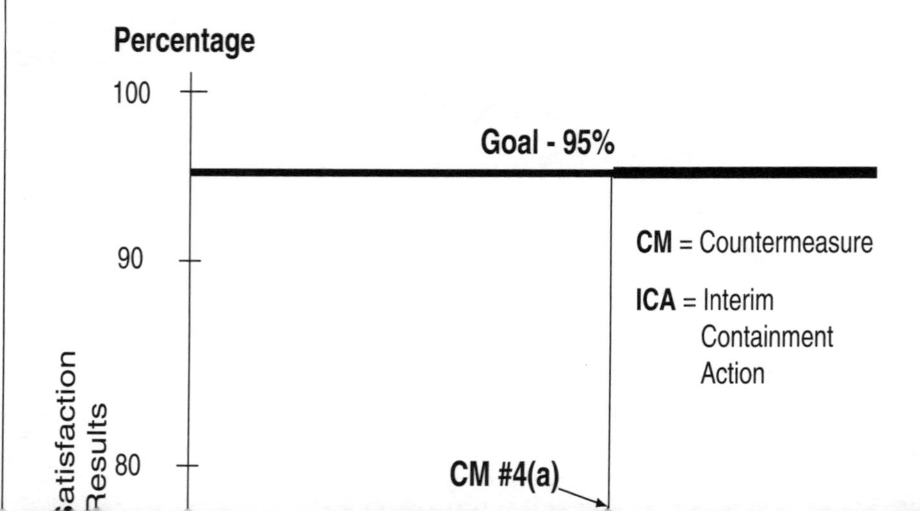
Percentage
100
90
80
Goal - 95%
CM = Countermeasure
ICA = Interim Containment Action
CM #4(a)

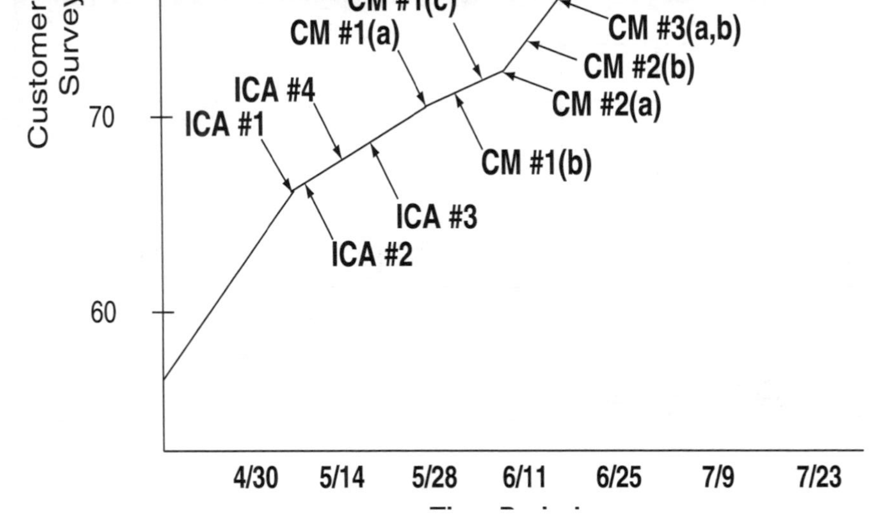
Customer Survey
70
60
4/30
5/14
5/28
6/11
6/25
7/9
7/23
ICA #1
ICA #4
ICA #2
ICA #3
CM #1(a)
CM #1(b)
CM #2(a)
CM #2(b)
CM #3(a,b)

Standard Work Guidelines Worksheet

Note: If process cycle times need to be improved, consider using the Standard Work Combination Table.

No.	Process Name	ICA or CM#	Flowchart Available	Process Owner	Training Completed	Measurements in Place
1.						
2.						
3						
4.						

5.					
6.					
7.					

Standard Work Guidelines Worksheet

Note: If process cycle times need to be improved, consider using the Standard Work Combination Table.

No.	Process Name	ICA or CM #	Flowchart Available	Process Owner	Training Completed	Measurements in Place
1.	New Sales program	CM #1(b)	Yes	K.W.	Yes	Yes
2.	CSRs work loads - order entry	CM #2(c)	Yes	B.K.	Yes	Yes
3.	New fulfillment system process	CM #3(b)	Yes	J.I.	Yes	Yes
4.	On-line checklist	CM #4(a)	Yes	J.I.	Yes	Yes

5.						
6.						
7.						

Performance Measurement Worksheet

1. Describe the need for this performance measurement.

2. Describe the activities (containment actions, countermeasures) planned to address the need.

3. How many people will participate in each activity?

4. When does the activity begin?

5. When does the activity end?
6. What are the targets and where are they posted.
7. Describe how the data will be collected. Frequency and by whom?
8. Combine your anticipated results and your targets in 1-2 sentences.

Performance Measurement Worksheet

1. Describe the need for this performance measurement.

   Incorrect invoices have a direct impact on the Customer Satisfaction Survey, as well as profitability and cash flow for the organization.

2. Describe the activities (containment actions, countermeasures) planned to address the need.
   1. CM#1(c) will ensure proper discounts are credited to all invoices.
   2. CM#3(b) will ensure orders are not shipped short, and if so, invoice will reflect actual shipment.
   3. CM#4(a) will ensure orders and invoices over $5000 are correct.

3. How many people will participate in each activity?
   1. CM#1(c) assigned to J.B.
   2. CM#3(b) assigned to J.I.
   3. CM#4(a) assigned to J.I.

4. When does the activity begin?

1. CM#1(c) 5/30
2. CM#3(b) 6/1
3. CM#4(a) 6/1

5. When does the activity end?
    1. CM#1(c) 9/30
    2. CM#3(b) 9/30
    3. CM#4(a) 9/30

6. What are the targets and where are they posted.
    1. CM#1(c) Reduction in invoicing errors by 33%; posted on Acct. bulletin board
    2. CM#3(b) Reduction in invoicing errors by 33%; posted on Acct. bulletin board
    3. CM#4(a) Reduction in invoicing errors by 33%; posted on Acct. bulletin board

7. Describe how the data will be collected. Frequency and by whom?
    1. CM#1(c), manual review daily, C.M.
    2. CM#3(b) 9/30, manual review daily, C.M.
    3. CM#4(a) 9/30, manual review daily, C.M.

8. Combine your anticipated results and your targets in 1-2 sentences.
   Each of the three CMs most likley will reduce the 8% invoice errors to <2% within a three month period. The CMs will also increase the survey results to 90+%.

Yokoten Worksheet

Problem:__________________________ **Presentation Date:** ____________

List team members that will present at Yokoten meeting.

Convey pre- and post measurements in simple form.

Place a check mark (✓) by each waste that was eliminated.

	Overproduction		Overprocessing
	Waiting (Queues)		Inventory
	Motion		Defects
	Transport		People's Skills

Convey timeline in simple bar graph form.

Place a check mark (✓) by the tools used. Identify the main tools used by placing a cirlce around each check mark.

	5S		Effective Meetings		Idea Kaizen		Perf. Measurement		Takt Time
	5 Why Analysis		Effective Team		Impact Map		Pitch		Training Plan
	Accepting Change		Failure Prev. Analysis		Just-In-Time		Problem Identfication		Value Stream Mapping

	Brainstorming		Fishbone		Kanban		Pull Systems		Waste Audit
	Continuous Flow		Flowchart		Mistake Proofing		Run Chart		Work Load Balancing
	Cycle Time		Gantt Chart		Paper File System		Runners		Yokoten
	Data Collection		Heijunka - Leveling		Pareto		Standard Work		

List any Idea Kaizens that were generated.

1.
2.
3.

List recommendations to management.

1.
2.
3.

List a few experiences regarding the four stages of team development.

1.
2.
3.

List recommendations to other teams.

1.
2.
3.

List overall benefits from the PDCA Kaizen Event.

1.
2.
3.

List contact person and email for additional information.

List where the electronic version of the Yokoten, as well as the supporting materials, are located for future reference.

Yokoten Worksheet

Problem: Incorrect invoices accounting for negative trend in Customer Satisfaction Survey results

Presentation Date: 9/1

List team members that will present at Yokoten meeting.

Jeff (IT), Juan (HR)

Convey pre- and post measurements in simple form.

Pre - 8% of all invoices incorrect
Post - <2% of all invoices are incorrect
Pre - 55% cust. sat. level
Post - 95% cust. sat. level

Place a check mark (✓) by each waste that was eliminated.

	Overproduction	✓	Overprocessing
	Waiting (Queues)		Inventory
✓	Motion	✓	Defects
	Transport		People's Skills

Convey timeline in simple bar graph form.

		May	June
Permanent Countermeasures (#1a and #4a)			
Update fulfillment system	20 days		
Create on-line checklist	10 days		

Place a check mark (✓) by the tools used. Identify the main tools used by placing a cirlce around each check mark.

	5S	✓	Effective Meetings	✓	Idea Kaizen	✓	Perf. Measurement		Takt Time
(✓)	5 Why Analysis		Effective Team	(✓)	Impact Map		Pitch	✓	Training Plan
	Accepting Change	(✓)	Failure Prev. Analysis		Just-In-Time	(✓)	Problem Identfication		Value Stream Mapping
✓	Brainstorming	(✓)	Fishbone		Kanban		Pull Systems		Waste Audit

	Continuous Flow	✓	Flowchart		Mistake Proofing	(✓)	Run Chart		Work Load Balancing
	Cycle Time		Gantt Chart		Paper File System		Runners	(✓)	Yokoten
✓	Data Collection		Heijunka - Leveling	(✓)	Pareto	✓	Standard Work		

List any Idea Kaizens that were generated.

1. Create on-line check list for quotes
2. All orders follow same process, no exceptions
3.

List recommendations to management.

1. More training on Lean tools
2. More of same type of events to improve processes
3.

List a few experiences regarding the four stages of team development.

1. Orginally thought it was all IT's problem
2. Sales very helpful in creating new on-line system
3.

List recommendations to other teams.

1. Ensure problem is clearly identified
2. Each team member to receive at least one action item
3.

List overall benefits from the PDCA Kaizen Event.

1. Achieved goal
2. Process permanently improved
3. All team members felt they contributed

List contact person and email for additional information.

Jeff Ito, IT, 745-665-1212, jeff.ito@tinkertowninc.com

List where the electronic version of the Yokoten, as well as the supporting materials, are located for future reference.

All forms, worksheets for this project are located: H:Yokoten/May_CustomerSurveyImprovements

Idea Kaizen Forms

The following pages contain the Idea Kaizen forms for you to use throughout your Kaizen Event. This form is included in the Kaizen Forms and Worksheets Microsoft Excel package available at
www.theleanstore.com.

Idea Kaizen Form

Name:____________________ Department:____________________

Upstream Customer:____________________ Downstream Customer:____________________

Step 1: Describe the Problem. Date:__________

Include photos, charts, and graphs, if necessary.

Step 2: Describe the Action to be Taken. Date:__________

Include photos, charts, and graphs, if necessary.

Step 3: Follow-up. Did the Action Work? ❐Yes ❐No Date:__________

Include photos, charts, and graphs, if necessary.

Additional Notes:

Idea Kaizen Form

Name:____________________ Department:____________________

Upstream Customer:_______________ Downstream Customer:____________________

Step 1: Describe the Problem. Date:__________

Include photos, charts, and graphs, if necessary.

Step 2: Describe the Action to be Taken. Date:__________

Include photos, charts, and graphs, if necessary.

Step 3: Follow-up. Did the Action Work? ❒ Yes ❒ No Date:__________

Include photos, charts, and graphs, if necessary.

Additional Notes:

Idea Kaizen Form

Name:____________________ Department:____________________

Upstream Customer:________________ Downstream Customer:____________________

Step 1: Describe the Problem. Date:__________

Include photos, charts, and graphs, if necessary.

Step 2: Describe the Action to be Taken. Date:__________

Include photos, charts, and graphs, if necessary.

Step 3: Follow-up. Did the Action Work? ❒Yes ❒No Date:__________

Include photos, charts, and graphs, if necessary.

Additional Notes:

Idea Kaizen Form

Name:____________________ Department:____________________

Upstream Customer:_______________ Downstream Customer:____________________

Step 1: Describe the Problem. Date:__________

Include photos, charts, and graphs, if necessary.

Step 2: Describe the Action to be Taken. Date:__________

Include photos, charts, and graphs, if necessary.

Step 3: Follow-up. Did the Action Work? ☐Yes ☐No Date:__________

Include photos, charts, and graphs, if necessary.
Additional Notes:

Case Study Lean Tools Update

The following Lean tools were used in the Tinker Town Kaizen Event.

Value Streams and Distribution Report

It was determined that the incorrect invoices were reflected throughout all customer orders. The team created a Distribution Report to delineate the three value streams that comprised all invoicing and the work that was associate with each one. There were additional value streams in administration and manufacturing, however, only these three were related to the problem.

Distribution Report

Department: Customer Service   Date: January 1 - March 31

Value Streams	January	February	March	Total
Orders - domestic	2140	2328	2012	6480
Orders - international	344	266	248	858
Quotes - domestic	146	158	178	482

Takt Time

The Orders – domestic value stream has a 5 minute takt time. The 5 minutes represents how often customer orders are arriving.

Available hours of operation: M-F 8am – 5pm = 9 hours/day (CSRs staggered lunches)
Total hours for one week = 45 hours
Twelve weeks Jan-Mar (average) x 45 hours week = 540 available hours per three month period.

$$\text{Takt time} = \frac{\text{Available daily work time}}{\text{Total daily volume required}} = \frac{\text{Time}}{\text{Volume}} \frac{(T)}{(V)}$$

$$\text{Takt time} = \frac{\text{540 hours or 32400 minutes}}{\text{6480 domestic orders}} = \text{5 minute takt time}$$

The takt time for Orders Intl is 540 hours or 32400 minutes / 858 = 37.76 or approx. 40 minutes.

The takt time for Quotes – domestic is 540 hours or 32400 minutes / 482 = 67.22 minutes or approx. 70 minutes.

This information assisted the team in determining exactly how much work was being done by the customer service department.

Continuous Flow with FIFO Lane

It was realized that a true pull system could not be attained in this situation, however, a FIFO (First-In First-Out) Lane was used to ensure all orders were processed in a timely manner from Sales to Customer Service to Shipping. Also, having the Intl orders updated regularly greatly assisted the flow of information. This resulted in the customer service department working less overtime and thereby reduced the likelihood of a data entry error on an invoice. The following illustrates the work flow of the orders.

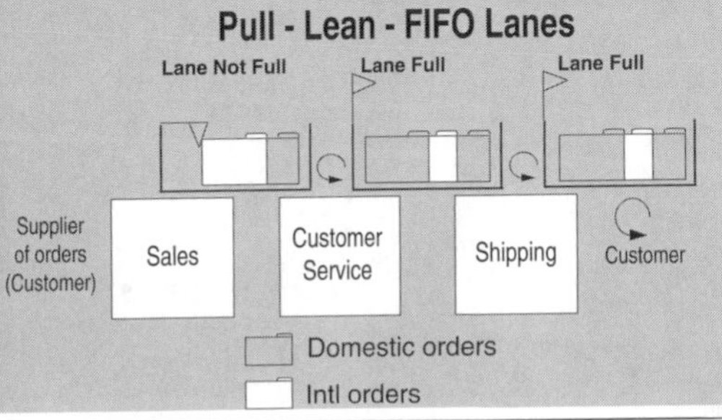

Standard Work

Standard work will come in all shapes and sizes. The illustration shown on the adjacent page is the fulfillment system standard work procedures. They used a Just-In-Time symbol to represent immediate information flow to the next step or process. The stop signal represents a delay in that some conditions must be met. Be creative when you create your standard work procedures. This particular form assisted the team in the orders that were being shipped short. Now those orders being shipped short had the correct price reflected on the invoice.

Standard Work Procedures Customer Ordering w/ Discount			
Item	**Activity Description**	**Responsibility**	**Process Symbol**
1	Place information from order into gateway	IT	
2	Index Team record date, value, customer name, customer code, and release to queue	CSR	
3	Order is picked off queue by CSR		
4	Check RFS to see if customer has existing file		
5.1	Do a search on Opening Screen to confirm customer ID is on file		
5.2	A Select the copy customer info on both Screens, or		JIT
5.3	B Select cancel option on both Screens, or		
5.4	C Check current details, match auto populated details, or		
5.5	D Enter customer details on Screen 1		
5.6	If more than 1 customer, repeat steps 4 to 5.4		
5.7	Enter "0" in the number of company searches required (Screen 2)		
5.8	Enter details for multiple site shipments		
5.9	Complete all details on Screen 5 for each order		
5.10	Link discounts to orders on Screen 6		
5.11	Enter standard discount details for each order on Screen 6		
6.1	Validate and save information, then select process Screen which will trigger Credit Reports to be generated	Accounting	⃠
6.2	Close the Fast Trace Summary from process Screen. Press Edit on the process Screen to re-enter credit details		
7.1	Assess all supporting information in line with credit policy	Accounting	⃠
7.2	Confirm, update credit information for customer file		
7.3	Update Screen 2 with data from report generation		
7.4	Save and validate information. Review and email to CSR		
8.1	Conduct order fulfillment from Screen 4	CSR	JIT
8.2	Note! Check any special notes on top of screen		
8.3	Update order checklist on Screen 5		
8.4	Create pick list and submit to shipping on Screen 7		
9.1	Obtain customer pick list	Shipping	JIT
9.2	Fill order to pick list and ship. Use SOP 4.2 for shipping instructions		
	JIT Just-In-Time information - this denotes information is immediately processed once it is received ⃠ Hold - work cannot proceed until conditions are met	Takt time = 5 minutes	

Pitch

The pitch was determined to be 2 hours (takt time of 5 minutes multiplied by 24 domestic orders = 120 minutes) from sales to shipping. This time was initially set as a trial and further modifications would be made as the team went forward. Once pitch had been established for the orders – domestic value stream - then the other value streams could be added. However, it is recommended that one value stream be "Leaned out" before attempting to work on another one. The following illustrates pitch for customer orders.

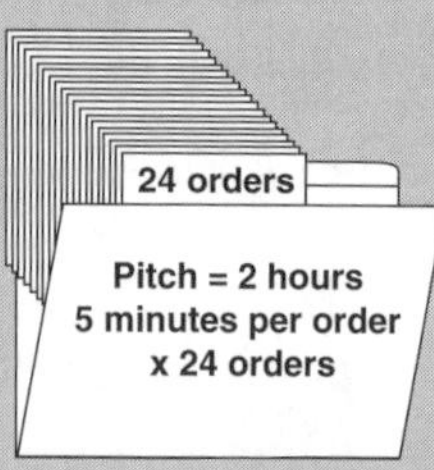

Work Load Balancing

The CSR department had territories assigned to each CSR. They created a Worker Balance Chart to better understand the various functions for international orders, which had an impact on the domestic orders. IT worked with CSR to streamline some of the credit checks so the CSR could initiate them as soon as the new customer for Intl orders were received. Cross-training was also a part of this work load balancing to alleviate the CSR work loads. The Intl orders and all quotes were creating backlogs for all orders, therefore, the team decided to balance the quotes as part of this Kaizen Event.

Worker Balance Chart Current State

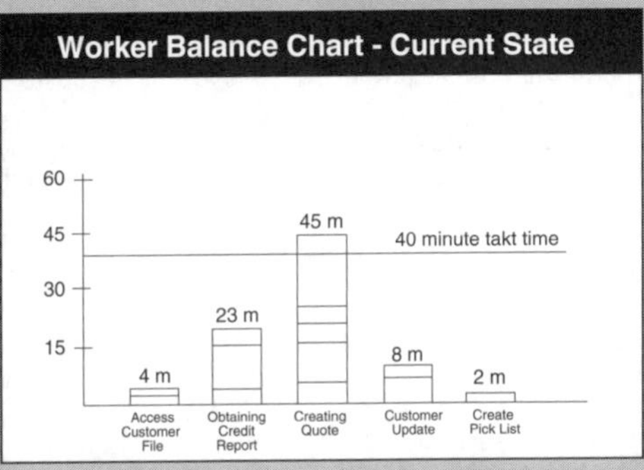

Worker Balance Chart Future State

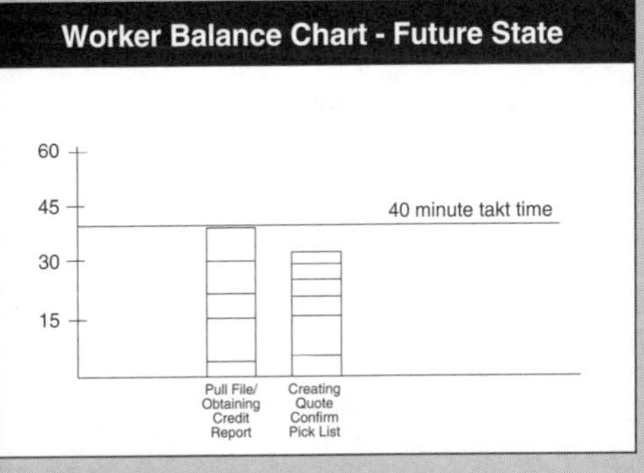

Mistake Proofing

IT created an automatic Sales update program that onc the discounts were entered by the Sales representativ (given certain conditions made by the Sales manage they would automatically be accessed by the custome service representative. They ensured that the discour that was quoted would be exactly what would be invoice (For 30 days they also checked each invoice to ensure th system worked.)

Visual Controls

The team created an on-line visual control system for cus tomer orders. It would not allow the Pick List to be prin ed unless all fields were completed. This ensured the dis count schedule would be checked to the customer I prior to fulfillment. Each CSR had a checklist that liste each of the customer requirements displayed on the screen. For each order, and as information was comple ed, a check mark would be placed in the appropriate bo along side the requirement. IT was a great help in provic ing this desktop tool for the CSR.

Kaizen Event Forms

The following four pages contain forms to assist you in the planning and reporting aspects of your PDCA Kaizen Event. These forms are included in the Kaizen Forms and Worksheets Microsoft Excel package available at **www.theleanstore.com.**

Kaizen Event Preparation Schedule

The Kaizen Event Preparation Schedule should be used by the Team Leader, Black Belt, or whomever is facilitating the continuous improvement event. The success of a Kaizen Event depends on the detailed planning that is done beforehand. Place a checkmark (✔) by those items that have been completed.

3 Weeks Before Event

- ❑ 1. Select area and topic.
- ❑ 2. Meet with Sponsor (Champion), Process Owner, and Financial Leader and any other key associates to:
  - Prioritize value streams that relate to Balanced Scorecard
  - Secure full time participation by team members for the event
  - Ensure Sponsor is availalbe for the kick-off meeting and the report outs (if applicable)
  - Discuss objectives and scope of the project
- ❑ 3. Ask these questions:
  - Will this team improve the process/functional performance?
  - Are the resources being focused on the right priorities?
  - What is the business case for analyzing and improving this value stream?
- ❑ 4. When filling out a Team Charter, ensure:
  - Facilitator is assigned
  - Additional expertise (i.e., Black Belt) is available (if appropriate)
  - Team member roles are defined (scribe, timekeepper, etc.)
  - Boundaries of the project are clearly defined
  - Customers of the process are clearly identified
  - Suppliers to the process or area are clearly identified
  - Dates have been established and agreed to
- ❑ 5. Secure conference room for the event. The room should be:
  - Located as close as possible to the process area that is being worked on
  - Available for the duration of the event
  - Large enough to conduct simulations (if required in the training)
- ❑ 6. Obtain all necessary supplies, such as:
  - Post-it Notes
  - Butcher paper ro..
  - Catering requirements
  - Flip charts and markers
  - Acess to copy machine
  - Materials (pocket guides, handbooks)
  - LCD projector
  - Copies of training
  - Snacks ☺

Deliverables

- ❑ 1. Team Charter created.
- ❑ 2. Metric/goal initially agreed upon.
- ❑ 3. Date(s) of the event determined.
- ❑ 4. Invititation sent to team members that includes date, location, event particulars and Team Charter.
- ❑ 5. All necessary supplies (training materials) have been ordered.

Comments/Notes:

Kaizen Event Preparation Schedule

The Kaizen Event Preparation Schedule should be used by the Team Leader, Black Belt, or whomever is facilitating the continuous improvement event. The success of a Kaizen Event depends on the detailed planning that is done beforehand. Place a checkmark (✔) by those items that have been completed.

2 Weeks Before Event

- ❑ 1. Review the 3 Weeks Before Event Checklist.
- ❑ 2. Gather date/identify sources that would be on a current state value stream map.
  - Obtain financials, flow charts, etc. of the process
  - Run reports of data of current process or collect real time (if applicable)
- ❑ 3. Determine current customer steady state demand (takt time).
- ❑ 4. Determine key individuals needed to support the event as on an ad hoc basis (facilities, IT, HR, etc.). Communicate to them appropriately.
- ❑ 5. Review Team Charter with Sponsor ahd Process Owner. Discuss schedule, measurements, targets, and deliverables on the proposed event.
- ❑ 6. Review Lessons Learned, Sunset Reports, Kaizen Event Evalution Forms from any previous events that may impact this event.

Deliverables

- ❑ 1. Team Charter completed and agreement reached on specific deliverables.
- ❑ 2. Sponsor scheduled for kick-off meeting and report outs.
- ❑ 3. Date(s) of the event determined.
- ❑ 4. All team members notified.
- ❑ 5. Data collection started or planned to be gathered.

1 Week Before Event

- ❑ 1. Review 3 Weeks Before Event and 2 Weeks Before Event list and resolve open issues.
- ❑ 2. Hold final preparation meeting with Process Owner.
- ❑ 3. Review metrics and goals with Process Owner for final agreement.
- ❑ 4. Update Team Charter, if necessary.

Deliverables

- ❑ 1. Team member participation verfied.
- ❑ 2. Team Charter released to all team members.
- ❑ 3. Materials acquired.
- ❑ 4. Room and catering verified (those snacks ☺).

Comments/Notes:

____

____

Kaizen Event Daily Review

The Kaizen Event Daily Review allows for a team to list their accomplishmentes, as well as their areas of concern, that should be reviewed by the Team Champion on a daily basis. Many times there will be a report-out at the end of the day in which all leadership of the organization are invited to attend. This review allows for immediate communication as to the project's status.

By: Date:

Team Name or Value Stream:

Measurements	Metrics						
	# Before	Day 1	Day 2	Day 3	Day 4	Day 5	Target

Accomplishments:	Concerns:	Plans:

Kaizen Event Scorecard

The Kaizen Event Scorecard is meant to regularily convey the results of the improvements. In doing so, it will provide the te with the necessary data in which to make corrections if trends are negative and the improvements are not going as expected. The Scorecard will also provide management with the improvement team's progress-to-date.

Event Name:	Site/Location:	Date:
Value Stream Impacted:	Process Owner(s):	Team Members:
Team Champion/Sponsor:	Team Leader:	

Measurements	Metrics							
	# Start of Event	# End of Event	7 Day Date: ____	14 Day Date: ____	30 Day Date: ____	60 Day Date: ____	90 Day Date: ____	Target

Overall Evaluation:

R	Y	G	R	Y	G	R	Y	G	R	Y	G	R	Y	G

Key:
- Performance Meets or Exceeds Target (Green)
- Performance is Short but close to Target (within 10% of Taget) (Yellow)
- Performance is Significantly Unfavorable to Target (below 10% of Target) (Red)

If the measurement is not meeting target(s) the below 3 W information (What, Who, and When) must clearly indicate how you plan to meet or exceed target.

What	Who	When	Comments/Status

Comments/Notes:

Glossary

5S - A process to ensure work areas are systematical kept clean and organized, ensuring employee safety an providing the foundation on which to build a Lean Office

5 Why Analysis - A method to assist a team in arriving a the root cause of the problem quickly without statistic analysis. The 5 Whys strategy involves looking at an problem and asking: "Why?" and "What caused this prob lem?" as many times at it requires to get to the root cause

ACT - The fourth phase of the PDCA Kaizen Event cycle It adopts and updates the necessary standards, aban dons the process change, or runs through the cycl again.

Activity - The single or multiple act of taking a course c action.

Assessment - A structured form upon which to analyze department or area relative to a particular topic.

Balance Scorecard (or Quality Dashboard) - A broa set of categories on which an organization is measure on. These measurements have goals and when a certai category is not meeting its goal, then resources (such a a PDCA Kaizen Event) are planned.

Basic flowchart - Standard symbols used to identify a the major steps in a process - usually no more than si steps. Mostly used for the 30,000 foot view for manage ment review.

Benchmarking - A structured approach to identify, visit and adapt world-class practices to an organization.

Brainstorming - The process of capturing people's ideas and organizing their thoughts around common themes.

Cause and Effect Diagram - A visual representation to of the various factors affecting a process.

CHECK - The third phase of the PDCA Kaizen Event cycle. It verifies results on actions taken to solve the problem.

Continuous flow - A process's ability to replenish a single work unit or service that has been requested or "pulled" from a downstream process. It is synonymous with Just-In-Time (JIT), which ensures both internal and external customers receive the work unit or service when it is needed, in the exact amount.

Check sheet - The visual representation of the number of times an activity, event, or process occurred for a specified time period.

Control chart - The visual representation of tracking progress over time. Similar to line graphs.

Countermeasure - The short and long term actions taken by the team members to isolate and eliminate the root cause(s) of the problem.

Cycle time - The time elapsed from the beginning of a work process request until it is completed.

Customer - The next process that requires something to be provided (i.e., data, information, service, material, etc.)

Customer demand - The quantity of product or service required by the customer. Also referred to as takt time.

Data - Factual information used as a basis for further analysis.

Data Check Sheet - A method by which to collect, organize, prioritize, and analyze data.

Deployment flowchart - Standard symbols used to visually convey the people (or departments) who are involved in the process. These flowcharts are helpful if the process being mapped crosses departmental boundaries.

DO - The second phase of the PDCA Kaizen Event cycle. It develops and implements solutions to a problem.

Document tagging - The physical attachment of a form to a process work unit to document dates and times.

Effective meeting - The efficient use of people's time when they are gathered together working to obtain a desired result.

Facilitator - A person designated in a meeting to ensure everyone stays on task and everyone contributes.

Failure Prevention Analysis - A technique that allows the Kaizen Team to anticipate problems before the implementation of a solution.

First-In First-Out (FIFO) - A work controlled method to ensure the oldest work upstream (first-in) is the first to be processed downstream (first-out). This could be a raised flag or an e-mail alert.

Fishbone diagram - *see Cause and Effect Diagram.*

Flow - The movement of material or information.

Flowchart - Standard symbols used to visually represent a type of operation, process, and/or set of tasks to be performed.

Forming - The first stage of team development. It involves reviewing the PDCA Kaizen project, establishing team roles, determining meeting times, and ensuring the right members are on the team.

Frequency Chart - A visual representation of the number of times an activity, event, or process occurred for a specified time period.

Gantt Chart - A bar chart type that visually represents the Interim Containment Actions, Permanent Countermeasures, and scheduled tasks, while depicting progress in relation to time. It is similar in nature to a timeline that denotes actions over time.

Heijunka (same as Leveling) - The balancing of work amongst the workers during a period of time both by volume and variety.

Heijunka box - A physical device to hold the work units arranged by value streams. It is similar to a group of mail boxes.

Histogram - The visual representation that displays the spread and shape of the data distribution.

Idea Kaizen - A quick and easy method to document and solve a "to-do-it-yourself" type problem.

Impact map - A method by which a team can identify the solutions that will most likely have the greatest impact on the problem with the least effort.

Individual cycle time - The rate of completion of an individual task or single operation of work; for example, obtaining a credit report for a mortgage application.

In-process supermarket - The control of work units in and out of an area residing between two processes to improve work flow.

Interim containment actions - The activities that wi immediately isolate the problem from your customer. Thi may require additional resources, manpower, etc. an many times is considered a band-aid until Permaner Countermeasures can be put in place.

Interruption - The stopping of a process without notice.

Just-In-Time (JIT) - Synonymous with continuous flow. is the provision that the process or customer is supplie with the exact product or service, with the right amount, a the right time.

Kaizen - “Kai” means to "take apart" and “zen” means t “make good". Kaizen is synonymous with continuou improvement.

Kaizen Event - A focused group of individuals dedicate to applying Lean tools to a specific area within a certai time period.

Kanban - A card or visual indicator that serves as means of communicating to an upstream process pre cisely what is required at the specified time.

Leveling (same as Heijunka) - The balancing of wor amongst the workers during a period of time both by vo ume and variety.

Metric - A specific number (data) that is utilized to meas ure before and after improvement initiatives.

Mistake proofing - The specific actions, devices, alarms etc. that are used in preventing errors from occurring c turning errors that have already occurred into defects *Also known as poka-yoke*.

Norming - The third stage of team development. At this point it involves that team ground rules are being adhered to, communication is occurring without disruptions, and progress is being made toward the objective. Everyone is contributing in a positive way.

Opportunity flowchart - Standard symbols used to display the process and categorize between the value-added from non value-added activities.

Pareto Chart - The visual representation in a bar chart format listing of issues in descending order of importance.

PDCA Kaizen Event - The use of the PLAN-DO-CHECK-ACT problem solving methodology tools (i.e., fishbones, pareto analysis, 5 Whys, countermeasures, etc.) with a focus on Lean.

Performance Measurements - The measurable indicators that can be systematically tracked to assess progress made in achieving predetermined goals and using such indicators to assess progress in achieving those goals.

Performing - The fourth stage of team development. It involves diagnosing and solving problems with relative ease, making constructive self-changes, achieving project milestones earlier than anticipated, and coaching other team members.

Permanent countermeasure - The activities that modify or create a process standard. These changes will ensure that the root cause(s) of the problem will not occur under similar circumstances.

Pitch - The adjusted takt time to move work units throughout the value stream.

PLAN - The first phase of the PDCA Kaizen Event cycle that identifies and analyzes a problem. It establishes the foundation upon which the team resources will be allocated.

Poka-yoke - It is Japanese for mistake proofing. It is derived from "poka" - inadvertent mistake and "yoke" avoid.

Problem solving - A team working together, following a structured process, to remedy a situation that caused a deviation from a norm.

Process - A sequence of tasks (or activities) to deliver a product or service.

Process flowchart - Standard symbols used to represent a process in detail. It will provide a detailed visual listing of all the major and sub-steps in a process.

Process mapping - Visual representation of a sequence of operations (tasks) consisting of people, work duties and transactions that occur for the design and delivery of a product or service.

Pull - A system in which nothing is produced by an upstream (supplier process) until the downstream (customer process) signals the need for it. This enables work to flow without detailed schedules.

Push - Work is pushed along regardless of need or request.

Queue times - The amount of time a work unit or service request must wait until it is released.

Resistance - The opposition of an idea or concept.

Root cause - The origin or source of the problem.

Run Chart - The visual representation of serial data points over time.

Runner - A designated function for someone to maintain value stream pitch integrity.

Scatter and concentration plots - The visual representation of data to study the possible relationship between one variable and another.

Scribe - A person designated in a meeting to take notes.

Set-In-Order - The second activity in the 5S system. This will ensure items are properly stored and placed in the correct location.

Shine - The third activity in the 5S system. This involves cleaning everything thoroughly and ensuring cleaning is part of the audit process.

Sort - The first activity in the 5S system. This involves the weeding out of items within the target area that have not been used for a period of time or are not expected to be used.

Spaghetti diagram flowchart - Standard symbols used to trace the path of a part, document (electronic), person, or service through all its phases.

Standardize - The fourth activity in the 5S system. This involves the creation of documents/rules to ensure the first 3 S's will be done regularly (and made visible).

Standard work - A set of procedures that control tasks that are executed consistently - without variation from the original intent.

Standard Work Combination Table - The visual representation displaying the flow of human work and all the various steps required to complete a process.

Standard Work Chart - The visual representation displaying the sequence, process layout, and work units for a process.

Storming - The second stage of team development. It involves team members realizing that the task is different and/or more difficult than they first imagined. Impatience about the lack of progress and inexperience on group dynamics has some team members wondering about the entire project.

Storyboard (A3 Report) - A graphically rich, visual representation of a Lean or problem solving project that displays critical information. Storyboards can be 8.5" x 11" or can be poster size.

Supermarket - The system of storing a certain level of in-process work or service capacity to be pulled by the downstream customer when there is a difference in the cycle times of the process(es).

Sustain - The fifth activity in the 5S system. This involves the process of monitoring and ensuring adherence to the first 4 S's. Many times this will be a regular audit.

Takt time - The pace of customer demand. Takt time determines how fast a process must run to meet customer demand.

Task - A single event within a process.

Team Charter - A document detailing the team's mission and deliverables to ensure strategic alignment.

Team leader - A person designated to ensure action items are evenly distributed and reports are submitted to the Team Champion as required.

Timekeeper - A person designated to ensure a meeting stays on track.

Timeline - A visual representation of key events within a particular time period, arranged chronologically.

Total cycle time - The rate of completion of a process or group of tasks that have a common element. It is calculated by adding up the individual cycle times for that process or value stream.

Training plan - The specific actions to educate the process workers on changes.

Value stream - A sequence of processes that are connected by a common customer, product, or service request.

Value stream mapping - The visual representation of the processes (work units and information required) to meet a customer demand.

Visual control - The visual indicators used to ensure a process produces what is expected, and if not, what must happen to remedy the situation.

Visual metric - The display of measurements.

Waste - Anything that adds cost or time without adding value. The seven most common wastes are: 1) Overproducing, 2) Waiting, 3) Transport, 4) Overprocessing, 5) Inventory, 6) Motion, and 7) Defects. Many times you will see an eighth waste added, that being 8) People Skills.

Waste audit - The method of analyzing a process in comparison to the seven (or eight) wastes.

Work load balancing - The distribution of work units across the value stream to meet takt time or pitch.

Work unit - A specific, measurable amount of work tha can be segmented and/or treated as a whole. Example of work units are: a customer order, a report, an e-ma request for information, or a bank deposit.

Yokoten - It means “best practice sharing” or “taking fron one place to another.” It encompasses the methods o communicating, documenting, and distributing knowledg about what worked and what did not work from a improvement project. It is a form of knowledge manage ment.

Index

D

E

F

G

J

K

L

M

N

O

P

R

Visit The Lean Store
www.theleanstore.com

for all your continuous improvement needs. Each month new products, books, videos, and worksheets will be made available as self-help tools for you to use!

Also, check out the Just For Fun section of the store.